Never Quit

A story of perseverance and love

By

To Melanie + Dave H

Robert Guliani

Life is good!!!

Robert Guliani

DEDICATION

To my best friend, companion, partner and soulmate Nydia. You make seeing the sun rise and set each day worth living for.

ACKNOWLEDGMENTS

Thanks to Nydia, my family, friends, classmates, colleagues and all those mentioned throughout the book that help make my life's bumpy journey a little smoother.

Thanks to my editors Steve Bellafiore and David Hellman for turning my gibberish into comprehensive sentences.

Thanks to my long time friend, Carmine Filloramo, for designing the front and back covers.

Thanks to my dear friend Barbara Taylor Bechtold for the excellent job of proofreading.

Finally, thanks to the Good Lord for giving me the time and strength to complete this book.

Prologue

It was a gorgeous mid-June morning in 1973 when a group of five friends decided to spend the day at Tobay Beach on Long Island, NY. The group consisted of three nineteen year old girls and two sixteen year old boys. After parking in the lot, everyone grabbed their gear and walked toward the beach, opened up their huge blanket and seized a bit of water front property. They were the first ones to arrive that morning and there was a feeling of tranquility in the air. The only sounds were those of seagulls scrounging for food and waves crashing on shore. With the temperature in the upper seventies, not a cloud in the sky, and a very light breeze, this was the definition of paradise.

The teenage girls immediately removed their street clothes and applied suntan lotion over their bodies before lying down on the blanket. They were eager to get an early start on their tans. The boys who had brought a football, began tossing it around. After thirty minutes of passing, catching and roughhousing the boys, now all sweaty and panting, dropped down on the blanket alongside the girls. When one of the boys suggested going in for a quick dip to cool off, he was instantly greeted with four emphatic no's!

Not to be discouraged, the one boy decided to go alone and test the water. The Atlantic Ocean doesn't warm up until late July on LI and the water was a frigid fifty-seven degrees on this day. As the boy trotted into the water, his four friends sat up to watch. He then dove with youthful enthusiasm through the first wave as he had done a thousand times before. For a few seconds all was as it should be and had been for the millions who swim in the waters off Long Island. Now instead of a triumphant reenactment of man conquering the sea, all they could see was the rise and fall of their friend's back floating face down in the surf. At first, they thought a joke was being played on them. Then, after a few seconds elapsed, they realized something had gone terribly wrong. In unison, as if spring loaded, they jumped to their feet and dashed down to the water to save their friend. The lifeguards, also spotting the swimmer was in trouble, leapt into the surf. Skillfully, they rolled him onto his back, thankful that he was still conscious, before gently maneuvering him toward shore and resting him on the dry sand. It was then that they realized that this boy, whose heart was pounding and gasping for air, could not move his arms or legs. He was paralyzed from the neck down.

The instant the boy's head had made contact with the wet sand changed his life forever. He was now facing a question that no sixteen year old boy should ever be asked. Whether to take arms against his sea of troubles and move on with his life or give up on life and suffer the slings and arrows of outrageous fortune. He chose to fight!

That boy was me and this is my story...

2

The common folklore is that when a person suffers a near death experience that their life flashes before their eyes and that there's a tunnel at the end with a bright light summoning them toward the afterlife. If you're lucky, your loved ones are on the other side waiting for you or urging you to turn back and return to earth because there is so much more that you need to accomplish to fulfill your life's purpose. I can report that none of the above happened to me. Instead what I experienced was a desperation to stay alive, to get my head above the water and to breath freely. There was an overwhelming heaviness weighing me down similar to what any person feels if he has challenged the ocean and found himself held down at the bottom under a massive swell. For me, that wave never lifted, there was no trough, there was no breaking from the water's hold on me, that is, until the lifeguards came along and rolled me on my back so that I could finally gasp for air.

In order to grasp the entirety of the story, it is necessary to get to know me before, during and after this "blink of an eye" life altering event occurred. So, let's rewind the clock, make yourself comfortable and let us get on with the story.

Chapter I - I'm here

It all started on an April morning in 1957, when a bouncing blond hair, blue-eyed, baby boy was delivered to the Guliani family. As their third and final child, I became the baby of the family and would never relinquish that title for the rest of my life. After a short stay at Glen Cove Hospital, it was time to head home with my parents, Richard and Dorothy, to meet my siblings. Home was located in a small town named Syosset, where I was greeted by my older brother Rick, and sister Susan. We lived in a red split-level house in a quiet working class neighborhood with families just starting out like ours. The house consisted of three bedrooms, two bathrooms and sat on a small grassy forty by one hundred foot lot. Many of my fondest memories occurred while growing up in that house and neighborhood.

Chapter 2 – The early years

It was the 1960s Parents of the baby boomer generation were fleeing the city to raise their families in the suburbs. The lure of green grass, fresh air, new schools and parks were too much to resist. Destination: Long Island.

Long Island is an off-shoot of Manhattan. It's surrounded on the southeast by the Atlantic and on the northwest by the Long Island Sound. LI extends one hundred and eighteen miles to Montauk Point, commonly known as *The End*. The town of Syosset is located near the center of the island roughly forty miles from NYC. The ocean is approximately thirty miles from our home and the Sound twenty miles to the north. To this day, Syosset and the surrounding suburban towns are an ideal place to raise a family with its excellent schools, parks, playgrounds and beaches. The world's greatest art galleries, museums, theaters and pro-sporting teams are all within reach in Manhattan, the Big Apple, through a short forty-five minute ride on the Long Island Rail Road. To this day, I still believe LI is one of the greatest locations to grow up.

As a member of the baby-boomer generation, we didn't have

all the electronic gadgets of today. Thankfully, the internet, laptops, video games, cell phones and social media hadn't been invented. We had to make do with one centrally located telephone in the kitchen where everyone could hear your conversations. If you wanted to make a personal phone call you had to find a phone booth somewhere in town and insert a thin dime. Instead of texting, taking selfies and playing video games, my friends and I always played outside no matter what the season. Our activities changed with the seasons. Whether it was playing baseball, football, basketball, soccer, swimming, riding our bicycles or anything else you can do outdoors, we were game for it. Weather permitting, on weekends, during summer vacation, and on holidays, we were on the go from 9am until 5pm when dinner called. The public parks were an extension of our lives. We never felt alone. They were always populated with kids of all ages playing unsupervised. In those days, life for kids was safe and simple, other than for the typical bruised elbows and knees, and hurt feelings if you lost a game of pick-up basketball. For today's youth, all I notice are empty parks and playgrounds. It makes me feel sorry that the good old days are long gone. What I would pay to be able to dribble a basketball one more time. Oh well.

Chapter 3 – Time for school

Upon entering first grade I quickly realized playtime was over. There were two possible schools where my parents could have enrolled me. There was the public elementary school South Grove, grades one through six or there was the parochial school St. Edwards, grades one through eight. Since St. Edwards hadn't been built yet, my brother went to South Grove; my sister went to parochial school and was part of the inaugural first grade class. All my friends were going to South Grove, just four blocks from the house. Allowing me no say in the matter, my parents decided to send me to parochial school...ugh!

The first day of school was frightening. I was a six year old boy wearing a shirt, tie, dress slacks and black shoes dragging my butt to the bus stop. Getting on the bus, my knees wouldn't stop shaking. As the bus pulled up to the school, we were greeted by all the nuns smiling ear to ear. I believe it was the last time they ever smiled, especially when it came to me. In all honesty I was a nice kid who always seemed to be in the wrong place at the wrong time.

First grade didn't start well. What kid, besides me, brings home a report card with a D in catechism from a Catholic school.

My parents were so mortified that they asked my Uncle Ed, a Catholic priest, for his advice. But even Jesus Christ couldn't help me. Sadly, this was just the beginning of my miseries.

At St. Edwards most of the students ate lunch at the same time. We would bring our paper bag lunch and buy a pint of milk in a cardboard milk container that you needed a surgeon to open. On the nice days, we were permitted to go outside for the remainder of our lunch hour. The play area was part of the church's parking lot with a section of grass in the far rear. All the girls would skip rope and play hop-scotch on the pavement. The guys would head straight to the back and onto the grass where we could finally release the pent-up anxiety of three hours of Catholic education under nuns probably trained in acts of torture. What quickly ensued was as close to a rumble as was legally possible without having to call the police. By the end of lunch many of us would return with ripped shirts, torn pants and scuffed shoes. It was all in good fun, of course. But the nuns couldn't see it that way. Each and every time we'd hear the same thing. "Your parents work very hard to buy you those nice clothes and now look at them." How could any of us really care after the psychological damage the nuns had done to us.

Fourth grade proved to be the only highlight of my parochial school education. It was announced that my teacher had an appointment after lunch and we were going to have a substitute. Normally when students see a substitute it becomes a green light to go crazy and ignore the rules. I was all geared up for the customary free-for-all when I learned that my mother was the substitute. Now what? As the volume in our room grew louder, I felt my embarrassment grow. This was my mother, not a stranger. Without thinking, I stood up and yelled, "Shut up." You could hear a pin drop. Everyone looked at me aghast. Then I explained to the class that this was my mother and anyone who wised-off would have to deal with me. The rest of the afternoon went smoothly and my mom never let me forget how proud she was of my actions. I had never realized before that I had the power to lead and how protective I could be; ready to take on the world when it came to family.

By the time fifth grade came my fantasies of greatness ended and I hit rock bottom. On a Wednesday afternoon my teacher, Sister Mary Ann, informed me that she wanted to meet with my dad Friday evening at 7pm. She was insistent that I relay that message to him. This was a grievous mistake. When I entered the classroom that Thursday morning she immediately asked for my father's response. I told her that my dad would be *delighted* to meet with her. How else would any eleven year old destined for hell respond? How could she know that I had lied. No one with his immortal soul on the line ever lied to a Catholic nun...oops! The weekend passed uneventfully, but on Monday, all hell broke loose. Sister Mary Ann informed me that she stayed up late into the night on Friday waiting for my father to arrive. Trust me, it was very hard not to laugh. I was beyond redemption and simply shrugged my shoulders and took my seat. Weeks passed with not a mention of my crime. I thought my plan had worked. I was a law unto myself. I didn't need the Ten Commandments to rule my life.

At home, the family weekends usually followed the same pattern. Saturday was yard work in the morning, and sporting activities in the afternoons. Sunday would start with morning Mass, then a stop at the store to pick up the newspaper, *Newsday*, and donuts or rolls. My mother would prepare a delicious breakfast and then my father would take us to the beach, weather permitting, or to visit with relatives. On one particular Sunday my dad stuck around to help with the collection offerings during the second Mass. Afterward, when he arrived home he said, "Guess who I met in church?" Before my mouth could utter a word he said, "Sister Mary Ann." My face turned ghostly white. "I'm going to meet with her Monday night." I gazed at the clock, knowing my freedom would end in thirty hours.

When Dad took off for his meeting, my friends and I were tossing the football around in the street. The fun abruptly ended when my dad returned home and summoned me home. Looking at his eyes and hearing the tone of his voice I knew it was futile to beg for fifteen minutes more to finish playing. The moment both my feet were inside the house, my dad yelled, "How could you lie to a nun?" Before I could invent an answer, a right hook glanced off the side of my head. My life flashed before my eyes as I stumbled down the stairs and pretended to be hurt. My punishment was severe. For the remainder of the school year, my sister would bring home my homework assignments and I had to carry home every book in my desk.

The light at the end of the tunnel came at the end of fifth grade when my sister graduated. The tuition policy at St. Edward's stated that the first child pays the full tuition and every other sibling attends for one dollar each. Now my parents were faced with a dilemma. If they wanted me to stay at St. Edward's it was going to cost them the full tuition. Knowing that paying for me was a waste of good money they asked me a rhetorical question. *Where would I like to attend sixth grade, public or parochial?* I quickly replied, "Public." To borrow a quote from Martin Luther King: "Free at last, Free at last, Thank God almighty I'm free at last."

Chapter 4 – Going public

For the first time in years, knowing that come September I would be attending South Grove made me actually look forward to school: a school with a gym, baseball and football fields and a swing set. No longer did I have to wear a uniform, or take a bus. Furthermore, I could attend classes with my buddies. More importantly, I had a chance to go to school with my longtime crush, Carole. She, who the nuns would have called *an occasion of sin*, was the cutest blond haired, blue eyed girl in the neighborhood. From the day she moved into the house directly opposite mine, I was smitten.

I was always good at arithmetic and knew that since South Grove consisted of three sixth grade classes with roughly twenty five students in each, I had a thirty-three percent chance of being in the same class as Carole. When we received the class assignments I sprinted to check which class she was in. *Eureka*, we were both assigned the same teacher. I was elated. Life was starting to look good again.

Our teacher was Mr. Cullire. He was a total breath of fresh air compared to my previous experience in Catholic school. He knew when to pat you on your back and when to gently tell you to chill out. He made learning interesting and fun which was all the motivation I needed.

There were two major events during sixth grade: one was the field trip to Washington D.C., and the other was getting Carole to say *yes* to becoming my first steady girlfriend.

The trip to D.C. was three days and two nights with the entire sixth grade, teachers and chaperones. We were assigned four classmates per hotel room. Ironically, I wound up with three juvenile delinquents whose idea of fun was throwing the glass ashtrays out the widow and watching them shatter in the parking lot. During the three days, we visited all the museums and landmarks. It was the most fun I had in a long time. Fortunately, my roommates didn't get me arrested. How different life had become in one short year.

It was around April that Carole finally said yes to me. We were at a classmate's party when I asked her to go steady. Carole didn't make it easy for me though. I had to kneel down and ask her for her hand. Then she hesitated for quite a while before eventually accepting. She was the first girl I ever kissed, kissed and kissed some more. Does anyone ever forget their first kiss? Their first love? To this day, we are still dear friends and keep in touch via email and social media.

On the final day of school, Mr. Cullire called me over. Looking me straight in the eyes he said, "Son, you are the nicest student I've ever had in my class." Wow, the prior year the nuns were calling me a devil and now my teacher saw me as an angel. I only wished we could have caught that scene on video so Sister Mary Ann could witness my transformation.

That summer before entering junior high we took a family vacation to the mountains of New Hampshire. My dad's company, Sperry Corporation, shut down for two weeks at the end of July and the family would always take a trip somewhere. We walked through caverns, hiked mountains and swam in crystal clear lakes. That vacation high was shattered within five minutes of returning home. A friend came running up to me to break the bad news. Carole was moving. Three months later she was gone. Yes, I was shattered and felt that my life was over. However, life does move on.

Chapter 5 – Junior High

Syosset School District consisted of fourteen elementary schools. It had two junior high schools: Southwoods and Harry B. Thompson (HBT). The schools were divided by a major road called Jericho Turnpike. If you lived on the north side of the turnpike you attended Southwoods; the south side HBT. Both junior highs then merged into Syosset High School.

This merger of schools had its positive and negative factors. The positive was the addition of classmates: more friends to meet and better competition on the sports teams. The negative was becoming the low man on the totem pole and having to adjust to the abuse the upper classmates would dish out.

My priorities in life had always been sports and girls. Education was a distant third. Seventh grade was my introduction to the game of soccer. I fell in love with the sport immediately. Besides my playing on both the soccer and basketball school teams, = seventh and eighth grade were uneventful.

To this day I am extremely competitive and a terrible loser. It hurts. This ranges from a competitive game in basketball to a game of Monopoly. Losing is not in my vocabulary.

Three things stood out in ninth grade. First, I had two girlfriends, Lori and Phyliss, but not at the same time. They were the first two girls I dated since Carole. Finally the drought was over. We were all going through those awkward teenage years with our raging hormones. It was the age teens start experimenting even if we had no clue what we were doing. Clumsy: definitely. Exciting: absolutely.

Second, ninth grade was my introduction to being hospitalized. While playing basketball at the local park I landed wrong and twisted my ankle. Initially, neither I nor my family took the injury seriously. I hobbled home and wolfed down my favorite dinner, homemade baked macaroni and cheese with pork chops. I nursed the injury with an ice bag to keep the ankle from swelling. But while watching the nightly news I suddenly felt nauseated and threw up my meal.

Still my family acted as if it was no big thing, that is, until a couple of days passed and my temperature began rising. The family pediatrician referred me to an orthopedic specialist who promptly admitted me to Syosset Hospital. The initial diagnosis was an abscess in the right ankle bone. The specialist prescribed x-rays, blood tests and five days of IV antibiotics twice a day with total bed rest. The adult room they had assigned me had an elderly man hooked up to numerous machines. With the constant noise, beeping, moans and groans, there was no way was I going stay in that room. The staff was kind enough to clear out an unused nursery and put an adult bed in for me. On the second day of my stay the specialist came in to take a biopsy. He explained that he was going to inject a needle through my ankle bone and remove some fluid. The purpose was to rule out blood poisoning. As he applied the Freon to numb the area my eyes caught a glimpse of the instrument that was he was using...OMG! He assured me that it wouldn't hurt and in went the needle. What a liar he was. It was the most painful thing I have ever felt to this day and my screaming was a testimony to that. The results came back negative, I finished my antibiotics and was discharged on the fifth day.

The third event came shortly afterward and proved to be a huge blow to my ego. I was the last player cut from the basketball team. This made me livid. After having a chance to settle down, I joined the town basketball league. The league was fun and it gave me the chance to shoot at will. One game, almost every shot I attempted went in. When the final buzzer sounded I had racked up forty-four points. The opposing coach walked across the court and asked me why I wasn't playing on the school team. He said if the school team had twelve players better than I it must be the best team in the country. The coach offered to contact the school coach to find out what was he thinking by cutting me. I appreciated him telling me this because he was also a part-time scout for the NY Knicks. He knew talent when he saw it. Later in the year, I crossed paths with the school coach and he apologized for cutting me. That took guts, but it was too little and way too late for me.

Toward the end of the school year our class organized a wheelchair basketball game between a traveling team and the teachers. The traveling team was comprised of paraplegics (paralyzed from the waist down) and amputees. They flowed up and down the court with such ease and little effort that the teachers had no chance. I left after the first quarter, not because it was a blow out, but for a shameful reason. Watching those paralyzed players terrified me. To this day, I'm not sure if it was a phobia that their paralysis might wear off on me or sadness at seeing these grown men unable to walk. Understandably, I kept this to myself. After my accident that following year my mind kept wondering if this was God's way of teaching me a lesson. Maybe one day I'll find out. But who knows? Ironically, it was the kind of fate that the good nuns threatened us with if they saw us making fun of anyone who suffered from a disability.

School remained an afterthought to me. With less than full effort, my overall average always ranged between B and B+. The only motivational factor to do well was to keep my parents happy so there would be no problems with me playing sports. My mother didn't raise a fool.

That summer we took a family vacation to Florida to drop my sister, Susan, off at Barry College in Key Biscayne, FL. Since my father loved to drive, before we dropped her off we stopped at Disney World. It was the second year of its inception and considered *the happiest place in the World.* The next day we arrived in Miami and spent a few days splashing in the warm waters of the Atlantic. After getting my sister settled in her dorm we were back on I-95 heading home. There was nothing more boring than the twelve hundred mile drive home, but it gave me time to think about how I was going to adjust to high school life. Two days later it was time to find out.

Chapter 6 – Penthouse

I didn't feel the usual first day jitters. While most of my classmates had an anxious expression on their faces, I was all smiles. Having played sports my entire life on school teams and in town organized leagues, I was already friends with a bunch of the students from Southwoods. With the merger of junior high schools we would now be united on the same teams competing for the same goals. Oh yes, there was one other reason for me to be happy: there was now going to be double the female student population. What red-blooded horny teenage boy wouldn't like that?

That first day, we all gathered in the main lobby. There was a lot of chatting with old friends discussing what we all did during our summer vacation. My eyes scanned the room and spotted this cute brunette sitting with my new school mates. I strutted over to the table where they were hanging out, and greeted those who I knew as I waited for my introduction to those I didn't. Right then and there my mind was thinking this is going to be a very good year.

As soon as the first period bell rang, we all scattered to our assigned classes. The first class was Spanish....Dios mios! Entering the classroom we all dutifully grabbed our seats. It was then that I noticed that cute brunette sitting by the window. I couldn't believe my luck. My friend informed me her name was Sue and I replied, "Gracias." Life was good.

Everything I could have expected from high school was realized in a hurry. But as we all know, nothing can go this smoothly. Of course, it soon ended. After homeroom it was off to biology where my smile faded fast when I glanced over at the teacher. Her name was Mrs. Fisher, a gray-haired old woman with very small lens glasses and a stare that would melt an iceberg. Biology classes ran for about fifty minutes, but every other day this class would run nearly two hours due to lab work. You can't imagine how much I dreaded these long sessions.

After labs, our assignment consisted of writing a lab summary. Nothing could be more boring. Mrs. Fisher, that witch, would grade them and hand them back the next day. As she was handing out the first lab summaries I could see A, A+, B, B-, A, A, A and one F. Of course, that was mine...ugh. My paper had so much red ink scribbled on it that it appeared her marker had exploded over it. This was going to be a very, very long year. I muttered a prayer and days later, as luck would have it, lightning struck Mrs. Fisher.

No, I didn't have to accidentally blow up the lab. This was even better because it didn't involve me. Coming back from gym class I spotted a teacher out cold on the floor. It turned out that a student running down the corridor collided with Mrs. Fisher.

Boom! Being a gentleman, I politely stepped over her prone body and sat at my desk, to await the good news. I would never dare be late. For the remainder of the school year we had a cool substitute. I would never wish ill-will on anyone but my happy life was back on track.

To add to my joy, I discovered that Sue was also interested in me. Socializing with the opposite sex came natural to me. Asking them on a date was a whole different story. Guys are always at a disadvantage because we usually make the first move which leaves our necks exposed to the chopping block. So, one day after class I mustered up all my courage and asked if she would like to come watch my soccer game after school. Sue smiled and politely said she would try to attend. I was giddy with excitement. My neck was still attached and I had avoided the pain of rejection.

During the soccer warmup my head kept turning to see if she was coming. But she wasn't in sight. It was only towards the end of the first half that I finally saw her waving to me as she sat in the bleachers. Sue stayed for the rest of the game. Together, we walked back to the gym. I took a quick shower, threw my clothes on and met her by the buses. She took a different bus so I politely asked if I could give her kiss. She nodded yes and we kissed goodbye. The outcome of that soccer game is still a blur to me. I won the only game that mattered.

Sue was a brown hair, brown eye cutie and a member of the cheerleading squad. She was about five foot three inches and couldn't have weighed more than a hundred pounds. We went steady for about five months, the first three of which were fabulous. As a couple, we went to concerts, school events and parties. The last two months of our romance turned into a chore, and I was never agreeable when it came to chores. Breaking up was the second hardest thing for me to do. But we both knew the magic had worn off and mutually called it quits. It was a good run while it lasted, but now I was a free agent again and the search was on for her replacement.

Soccer season was winding down and it was time for basketball tryouts. Basketball was my true love and I knew the competition was going to be fierce. I was roughly five foot eight and weighed one hundred and forty five pounds. So my size wasn't to my benefit. My hope was that my quickness and ball skills would push me into a spot on the team.

Lenny Mintz was the head coach of the team. There were twelve open spots and roughly ninety kids trying out. Coach was a short man with a muscular chiseled physique. He spent numerous hours pumping iron and it showed. Tryouts lasted two days and consisted of numerous basketball drills. He would walk around with his clipboard, writing his notes and crossing off names. At the end of the day a list was posted on a bulletin board and we all scampered to see if our name was still there. It was simple, if your name was on the list you would come back the next day, otherwise you'd come back the following year. I looked up and saw Rob Guliani....phew! For the next twenty four hours I could relax.

Day two wasn't as kind to me. After practice, we showered, dressed and raced to the bulletin board again. This time, as we all gazed up at the names one was missing, mine. It turns out I was last to be cut, which brought me no solace at all. We all piled on the bus for the drive home and my mates gave me some compliments and pats on the back for the great effort. But losing is losing. I didn't take it well.

As soon as the bus pulled up to my stop I jumped out and trotted home. The only thing on my mind was trying to figure out what went wrong. It was only the aromas of my mother's cooking that soothed my troubled mind. My family always ate dinner together, and if you weren't at the table on time you'd better have a good reason. Rules were rules in my household.

With both my brother and sister away at college, it was now just the three of us. There was no place for me to hide. My parents knew from the look on my face that tryouts didn't go well. Dad asked what happened and we talked it over, father to son. He said, "If you gave it your best then hold your head high and go on to your second option". He was right, of course.

Throughout life it's always nice to have multiple options in case your first option fails to materialize. This philosophy I have utilized successfully many times in my life. My second option was to play on the CYO (Catholic Youth Organization) team. It was a local team that practiced one night a week and traveled another night to different towns to play. Fortunately, on the day I got cut, CYO practice was being held that evening. This gave me little time to pout and feel sorry for myself. Right after dinner my dad agreed to drive me over. While we were still eating dinner the phone rang. My father, who never took kindly to interruptions, answered and said it was for me. It must have been important because my dad usually tells callers, we're eating; he'll call you back after dinner.

It was Coach Mintz calling to apologize. He said he made a grievous mistake cutting me and wanted me to show up for tomorrow's practice. I was shocked and exonerated. While I replied thanks, I knew the decision was now mine. It felt good to be back in the driver's seat for a change.

That night I attended CYO practice and informed the coach that the school team offered me a position and that I was going to accept it. In those years you were not allowed to participate on two traveling teams at the same time. The overriding factor for my decision came down to the ability to practice every day and improve my skills at the high school level. Playing against greater competition is a key to expanding your potential.

All said and done it was a good decision. Coach gave me enough playing time to keep me satisfied but by no stretch of the imagination was the team focused around me. There were some very talented players on the team and I quickly realized my role.

As practice ended that first Friday, Coach Mintz handed out copies of a massive playbook and asked the team to memorize them before Monday's practice. Reviewing it, I knew there was no chance in hell anyone, not enrolled in an Ivy League school, could comprehend it, let alone a bunch of teenagers. When Monday rolled around Coach called play number forty-three during a scrimmage. The five players on the court were clueless and he went ballistic. Looking back it was an excellent playbook. Unfortunately, youth is wasted on the young. After the playbook was condensed to a manageable ten pages, the team grasped the concept. We went on to have a good season.

Basketball season wound down that March and most of the winter athletes migrated to lacrosse or baseball. I wasn't really interested in either so I decided just to concentrate on other things. Sue and I were no longer an item so it was time to start looking again. Also, Coach gave everyone a report card summarizing our achievements, strengths and weaknesses, along with suggestions on how to improve in the off season. The number one item for me was to bulk up, which meant hitting the weights.

Chapter 7 – On cloud nine

As March turned to April everything was coming up aces. My brother's best friend, Phil, was going to visit him at Boston College, and he invited me to join him. Figuring there was no way in hell my parents would approve I didn't give it much of a chance. It entailed missing a day of school and trusting me to behave for three days without parental guidance. To my surprise my folks gave me the green light. I assumed they must have thought the college atmosphere would wear off on me and instill good habits.

That following Friday, Phil picked me up at my house. BC was a four hour drive which was out of the question. It was my first time on a plane and a bit unnerving. I now realized how the wealthy travel. We left LaGuardia and landed forty-five minutes later at Logan airport. We then hopped on the rail system for roughly eight minutes which left us within walking distance of the campus. Rick was already waiting when we arrived.

Rick shared a dorm with seven other guys. Even before I walked through the door my skin started to itch. What a pig sty. Empty bottles and beer cans were all over the place. Anything you touched stuck to you. Immediately, I began to miss my immaculate home. I don't believe this was the impression my parents were hoping for.

My brother had composed a fun-filled agenda for our stay covering many different activities. We started with a quick tour of the campus with special attention to the sporting venues and the student fitness center. The football stadium and fitness center was no more than two hundred feet from his dorm. Phil and I hadn't eaten since breakfast and were elated to hear that our next stop was dinner.

Dinner was at a restaurant named Durgin-Park. It's been in business for over a century and anyone who knows Boston has most likely dined there. They have a unique way of serving the patrons by dropping all utensils, napkins and dishes at the head of the table. It's then up to everyone, family-style, to pass everything down. The food was excellent and it was quite an experience. Leaving the restaurant, we walked around the town popping in to some local coffee shops to listen to live musicians perform.

Shortly after midnight we were back in the dorm and ready to crash for the night. Saturday started off with a game of pickup basketball and a quick swim at the fitness center. We then headed to the renowned Boston Garden to watch a NCAA men's hockey doubleheader. Five hours of hockey, four hot dogs and two beers later we were exhausted and headed back to the dorm.

On Sunday morning, we had a delicious breakfast at a small cafe and then left for Logan airport. Three hours later Phil pulled into my driveway. This was a great three day get-away, but there still is no place like home, sweet home. After briefing my folks, I took a nap.

The calendar now flipped to June which meant school would soon be closing and the end of the best year of my life was coming to an end. The last day of classes was scheduled for Friday, with finals beginning the following Monday. By that Thursday all our lockers were cleaned out and books returned to their appropriate places. The only purpose for school on Friday was to meet the state requirements. We were required to attend school for two hours. Fatally, I asked my parents if they would allow me to cut school to go to the beach with my sister's friends. They both nodded yes as long as I mowed the lawn and studied hard over the weekend for the upcoming finals. I replied, "You have my promise." It was only the second time in my entire life that I cut school.

That night I went to the community park to play some hoops and then to meet up with my sister's friends. I took the opportunity to beg one of her friends to let me try driving in the parking lot. She agreed. Sitting in the driver's seat, she began instructing me on what to do and then off we went. The car moved about five feet before my foot jammed on the brakes. That would be the last time I ever drove a car.

Everything in my life seemed set. I had already planned my summer vacation. I had obtained a job at a department store and registered for basketball camp. All I had to do was pass the finals and it was clear sailing. There is a saying, "Man plans and God laughs." In my case, it proved to be is so true.

Chapter 8 – D-Day

It was the fifteenth of June, 1973. This was my version of D-Day. This was the day the earth turned and the sun went behind the clouds. I went from being a healthy vibrant teenager with a world of promise and a pocket-full of dreams, to a paralyzed force that I could not break away from. The inability to move my limbs and the look on everyone's faces told me in no uncertain terms that I had screwed up royally. Everyone was telling me to relax as my heart continued to pound and even the simple act of getting air into my lungs became more laborious.

A stretcher was quickly located by the first-aid stand and my paralyzed body placed onto it. Immediately, I was transported to the first-aid area. The first aid workers stabilized my neck. In my mind, this was all temporary, something I would laugh about later with my family and friends. This was just a stinger. Like many sports injuries, you'll hit a nerve and a limb would go numb for a short period of time. Gee, was I delusional! But who wouldn't be?

Soon after, I heard the distant sounds of a helicopter getting louder and louder until it landed on the beach. The lifeguards and the police placed the stretcher inside the copter and began fastening the safety belts around me. The officer started hooking up a monitor to track my vitals and then placed a tube in my nose for oxygen. Then up we went. I had never been in a helicopter before. I learned that Syosset Hospital was our destination. For the entire flight, I was drifting in and out of consciousness. Every time my eyes closed the officer would yell, "Wake up. Stay with me." Where did he think I was going?

Upon landing we were greeted by members of the emergency room staff wheeling a gurney. Once secured, the gurney was wheeled rapidly into the ER where the staff swarmed around me. One nurse unhooked the officer's medical equipment while another nurse replaced it with the hospital's equipment. Everyone moved at warp speed. This is what they were trained for. The portable X-ray machine started taking pictures while another person inserted an IV and drew blood. Then a nurse cut off my bathing suit and inserted a catheter. When the orthopedic surgeon read the x-rays, he immediately had me placed in traction. Then a nurse asked if I had swallowed any ocean water to which I responded, "No." I was wrong and immediately proceeded to throw up half the ocean. I had nearly drowned, but didn't know it at the time. Everyone in the ER room knew their role and executed it to perfection. While all this work was being done on my body, not one person would tell me what was wrong and this was beginning to irritate me. I was petrified.

I was still trying to comprehend the extent of my injury, when my mom arrived. Hearing her screams and agonizing cries told me all I needed to know. *I screwed up big time*. This is the first time that expression truly made sense to me. My dad arrived shortly afterwards. Immediately, he was given the devastating diagnosis. He paused long enough to calm my mom down before they came in the room to see me. When they stood next to the bed railing, their eyes were red and watery. I had never seen my dad cry. This made me misty eyed. What could be that terribly wrong? He leaned over the bed railing and assured me things would be OK. He urged me to just concentrate on my breathing and *don't quit.* I quickly snapped back, "Quit is not in my vocabulary." We both smiled. He was my lifeline. While my mom stayed by my bedside whispering encouragement and saying an occasional prayer, my dad left the room to make some phone calls.

Dad was always the steady-handed, strong-minded member of the family. Come hell or high water he wasn't going to lose a child in a local hospital, not to criticize Syosset Hospital. What he accomplished in the next couple of hours, without the availability of modern cell phones, was amazing. Not only did he have to overcome the limitations of a pay phone, but he had to contend with the sad fact that in the summer months, between Memorial Day and Labor Day, Friday is getaway day for most doctors working in NYC.

Nothing was going to stop my dad from getting me the best treatment in the best hospital New York could provide. He started by calling his lifelong friend, Mike Pinto, a lawyer in NYC, to explain my situation. Mike told my dad he knew the head of Columbia Presbyterian Hospital who in turn recommended the top neurosurgeon at NYU Hospital. After all the arrangements were made, Mike called back to update my dad that a helicopter was on its way. Somehow I had gotten my second flight in a helicopter, but neither time had I had a window seat. Within forty minutes a copter landed and we were off to NYU.

While all this commotion was going on, my sister, Susan, arrived home from her summer job. When she noticed the lawn was uncut, she promptly headed toward the shed, she pulled out the lawn mower and made quick work of cutting the grass. My sister was protecting her baby brother from being punished for not completing his chores. That is the protective, caring person my sister is. Shortly after finishing, my parents informed her on what was transpiring and that I was in a lot bigger trouble than just neglecting my chores.

There were two heliports in NYC. One, was on the Eastside, over a thousand feet from the emergency room; the other on the Westside, clear across town. Of course, we landed on the Westside, and had to cross the city in an ambulance on streets full of pot holes and manhole covers. The driver hit every one of them. Sirens blaring, the ambulance bounced and swerved in and out of the lanes while my parents held tightly onto the stretcher. Just what we all needed.

When the ambulance doors swung open, there was Mike to greet and escort us. If you're lucky, there may be a dozen or so people you'll meet that will leave a lifelong positive impression on you. For me, Mike is one of them.

Chapter 9 – I.C.U.

Three NYU staff members were waiting at the ambulance bay to assist the EMTs into the waiting elevator. Then one of the EMTs started rattling off my vitals to the head nurse during the ride up to the fourteenth floor. When the door opened, they promptly moved me right into the intensive care unit, parking me next to the window by the nursing station. On the count of three, all five of them transferred me from the gurney onto a hospital bed before the EMTs scattered. There were three other patients in the room, all with brain abnormalities. During my seventeen day stay, I was the only one who would leave alive.

The neurosurgeon came in to discuss the situation with my parents and to explain the next steps. As they gazed at the x-rays, the doctor explained that since I had fractured my C3-C4 vertebrae, he needed to perform exploratory surgery to insure no bone chips were floating around that could cause even more damage. Aware that this doctor was one of the world's best, my parents agreed and promptly signed all the consent forms. The surgery lasted six hours with no major issues.

After the exploratory surgery, the neurosurgeon recommended

that the two vertebrae be fused together. This procedure would have stabilized my neck allowing me to start sitting months sooner than if it were left up to nature to heal. My parents declined since they felt I had gone through enough trauma. In retrospect, knowing how long the recovery period was, I'm not sure that would've been my choice. My parents did what they thought was best for me at the time.

Friday turned into Saturday. Every hour a member of the medical team would pull out their trusty pin. Then, they started sticking me on the chest and asking me, "Can you feel this? Here, here, how about here?" That's how the extent of the paralysis is gauged. If the lack of feeling moves upward, it indicates your lungs will now be compromised and that could be fatal. If it stays in the same area, which was my case, this means you're stable. Lower is what everyone was hoping for, but for me that wasn't to be. The staff explained that not until all the swelling subsided around the spinal cord would we learn what motor function would return.

This is when *the real fun* began. A guy wearing green scrubs came to my bedside and said he was here to shave my head. Grimacing at the guy I said, "When hell freezes over, you are." The last twenty-four hours weren't exactly going my way. If I was going to die, it wasn't go be with a bald head. The attendant explained they needed to shave the area so the neurosurgeon could implant the bolts that would be wired to the traction weights. Needless to say, I thought he was nuts. Then the neurosurgeon walked in and asked the attendant why he wasn't done yet. After explaining my refusal, we all agreed to a compromise. Little circles of hair where cut where the bolts were going to be screwed. The rest of my hair remained unscathed. My dignity was preserved even though I must have looked like something out of a science fiction movie. Hello, Dr. Frankenstein.

On Sunday morning, I got this weird sensation throughout my body. Lying flat on my back, I felt as though my head and feet were on the bed while the rest of my body was on the floor. Feeling like a piece of Silly Putty, I called the nurse to explain this sensation. She pulled the top sheet off and assured me everything was still on the bed. Unable to see for myself still left me with an eerie feeling. The nurse could sense I wasn't buying her assessment so she walked back to her station. A few seconds later, she came back with a pair of glasses and said let's try these on. They were prism glasses which allowed me to look up vertically while providing me with a horizontal view. I could now see my entire body. I stared at my paralyzed body for over an hour. Each minute was spent concentrating deeply while attempting to wiggle my toes or move my fingers. Praying each time that I would see some sign of life. But, to no avail. It was very depressing to comprehend the extent of my injuries.

That evening, my dad brought my best friend, Joseph Maneri, to visit me. On their commute in, he explained what Joseph could expect to see and how necessary it was to control his emotions. My dad entered the room first and we discussed that day's events. He asked if I was up too seeing Joseph and I quickly replied, "Of course." God had stripped me of many things, but he left me with my sense of humor. It is an attribute I have used many times to defuse awkward and tense situations. Joseph timidly walked around the bed until we eventually made eye contact. One look told me the whole story. He was devastated and it showed on his ghostly face. I immediately said, "Guess I should have hung out with you on Friday." He painfully eked out a small grin and replied, "Yep." The ice was broken and we had a pleasant visit. When Joseph exited the room, my dad came back to say goodnight. I asked him to try to ease Joseph's anguish on the ride home. He said no problem and then he kissed me goodbye. I honestly felt worse for putting my best friend though such a horrific ordeal than by my own predicament. It left me one unanswerable question. How would I have handled the situation if the roles were reversed?

My head was starting to clear by Monday morning when I heard a group of teens yakking in the hallway. The voices sounded like my classmates, but I knew they were all taking finals. Next thing I knew, twenty or so classmates were at my bedside. The ICU staff is usually very strict regarding the number of visitors, but the nurses must have assumed it would boost my moral. Wrong! It was emotionally overwhelming and left me very uncomfortable. When one of my friends remarked that the state final exams had been stolen and that the school year was officially over, I stared at the ceiling, in disbelief. I asked God, "Can you give me a break?"

After that, anyone visiting was always screened by my dad. He would prepare that person on my appearance and ask them not to cry or freak out. Not that he cared about the individual's feelings, but rather he didn't want me getting depressed. Dad was just protecting his *baby*.

Somehow, one evening my dad's screening failed when coach Mintz walked into the room. Coach was a physical education teacher and well aware of the human anatomy. He had a good grasp of my condition. As he approached the bed, his eyes were all red and he appeared nervous. His voice cracked as he spoke encouraging words. He then reached behind his neck and unclasped his gold chain that had a charm of the Torah attached. Gently placing it on my chest he told me he didn't want it back until I could hand it to him. After he left, I started to realize for the first time the magnitude of my injury and a few tears trickled out of my eyes. Then I quickly rationalized the situation and felt this was something that could be beaten. Maybe it was going to take longer to overcome than first imagined, but since I was in great condition and had a competitive spirit, I believed it was doable. Call it denial or naivety, but teenagers feel invincible. I was no exception to the rule.

On day seventeen, the medical staff determined I was stable enough to be transported to a rehabilitation center. In all the war movies, the wounded soldier always goes to a tropical island to recuperate. So, I was thinking Bahamas, Bermuda maybe the Virgin Islands. Sadly, it was an elevator ride down to the second floor through a main door with a sign that read Rusk Institute.

Chapter 10 – Rehab

Rusk Institute is a six story building attached to NYU, located on 34th Street in Manhattan, widely acclaimed in the medical field for its specialty in rehabilitation medicine. The first floor was for the adults and the fourth floor for children. My room was on the first floor and was shared with three others. The entire floor was comprised of roughly twenty-six rooms divided equally between men and women. The nursing station was located in the center, separating both genders.

My three roommates all had spinal cord injuries: one from a car accident, another from a motorcycle accident and the other one from a fall off a ladder. Once my bed was locked in place the parade began. The rehab doctor assigned to my case came in to introduce himself. One by one, the nurses and staff members followed. The head nurse was quick to point out that I was the youngest patient ever to be admitted on that floor. Then she suggested I get a good night sleep because therapy started the next morning.

My room was directly across the hall from the aides' room.. Since this was summertime in NY, they kept the windows constantly open. This let in quite a few flies that found their way to my bed. If you want to know what torture is like, try lying in bed with no motor function in your arms and a fly buzzing around your face. After a few minutes of this nonsense I cracked. I collected a lot of saliva in my mouth and the next time a fly landed near my mouth it got soaked and drowned. As the proverb says, "Necessity is the mother of invention." Welcome to my world.

The first few months my parents would come in every night after work. We'd discuss the events of the day. If anything was bugging me my dad would handle it. He went ballistic when he learned about the fly situation and immediately called the administrator who promised to take care of it. Days passed, but the windows remained open. One night, my dad took matters into his own hands. He hung fly paper all around the sink. The next morning when the chief of staff went to wash his hands, he walked directly into the fly paper which stuck all over his white shirt. He was livid. The aides' windows were never left opened again. You don't mess with the alpha dog, my dad.

Now that the Rusk Institute was going to be my home for the next nine months, I wanted to make sure the entire staff liked me. The golden rule for establishing a good patient-staff relationship is to compliment everyone and make them laugh. With my charm, I discovered that the nurses and therapists were very easy to win over. The aides, however, were more challenging. They viewed me as a spoiled silver-spoon baby, which was far from the truth. But once I rapped sports and trash talked back to them, everything was cool. Having learned enough Spanish in class proved helpful for me in bonding with the Hispanic staff. Once I had gained acceptance from everyone, I was all set.

When the morning came around, my physical therapist, John Merrick, walked in and introduced himself. He was a six foot three inch Vietnam vet, who had played linebacker at a small college, and grew up in the Boston suburbs. We hit it off right from the beginning. He told jokes as he stretched my arms and legs up and down constantly in order to prevent atrophy of the muscles and joint tightness. Using a protractor, he measured my range of motion and wrote his findings in his notebook. At this stage my only movement was the ability to shrug my shoulders. John finished up and said he'd be back at the same time tomorrow.

After being fed lunch, two gentleman from the prosthetic department walked in, and explained that their job was to construct a body cast for me that would allow me to sit up. They started by pasting this sticky stuff across my chest that they peeled off a few seconds later with an impression of my chest. Then they repeated the same process for my back. Both seemed pleased and they scooted off to their lab to produce my cast.

They came back the next day to try on the two piece body cast. Now picture this, the back piece ran from the lower portion of my back to behind my head with a strap that went around my forehead. The front was from my belly button to my chin. Then the two sides were strapped together turning me into a mummy. It was a killer and only allowed my mouth to open wide enough for a straw to fit in. Using their markers, they began circling the areas that needed to be fixed or padded. Tomorrow would be lift off, as I referred to it, when I would be placed in a sitting position.

The next morning, John Merrick, along with two aides, a nurse and the two guys who had built the body cast walked into my room. They brought with them a worn-out looking wheelchair that had seen better days. One of the prosthetic guys demonstrated how the cast went on, then fastened all the straps. Then the four others hoisted me up and into the chair. As soon as my butt landed in the chair I became very light headed. The only thing preventing me from blacking out was to tilt the chair back so the blood could flow back in my head. For the next four months, every time I got up the dizzy spell followed. I always tried to have a nurse tilt me because women had *fluffier pillows* than men for me to rest against. Boys will be boys.

Once I was able to sit, they started me on a daily regimen. The days of laying around and socializing with the staff were over. It was now time to get busy regaining some strength and flexibility. I was washed, dressed, fed and in the chair by 9 am. Nine to ten was physical therapy with John. Ten to twelve was school time with the tutor. My dad, always thinking ahead, realized how important it would be for me to graduate with my high school classmates. The tutor had a small classroom on the far end of the fourth floor. This was mainly the children's floor. Here, I observed something that would change my outlook on life forever.

Kids, ranging in age from four to thirteen, were playing a game in the hallway. They were laughing and all had a huge smiles. These kids, who had never walked a day in their lives and had a limited life expectancy, radiated happiness. I realized that I had sixteen great years enjoying life to the fullest, sixteen more than these kids would ever have. God's truth, from that day on I never shed one tear for myself or muttered *why me?* My philosophy became, no matter how bad my situation, there is always someone worse off.

Lunch was exciting, not because of the food, but rather because it meant getting back in bed so that the cast could be removed. That cast always dug painfully into my boney shoulders, one of the few areas I had sensation. Lunch hour always went quickly and I was back in the wheelchair for an hour of occupational therapy and two more hours of physical therapy. Four o'clock was the end of the day and back to bed for some rest and relaxation.

After a quick nap, dinner would be served. Shortly after that my parents and possibly a friend would arrive. After chatting for an hour or two, they would leave and I was done for the day. Saturday and Sundays were when most of my friends would visit since there was no schedule to follow. I'd get in the chair and we'd stroll around the hospital, or just hang out in the lounge and yak the day away.

Finally, after five weeks, on a Sunday afternoon, I tried moving my right arm and discovered that it moved slightly. Then my left arm showed similar results. Throughout the entire weekend I must have moved them a thousand times. I was fearful that if I stopped, this new found ability would fade away. That morning when John started my therapy I asked him what was that on my arm. When he got right next to it to get a closer look I smacked him. He was so elated, he almost peed in his pants. Then he said, now we can really get to work.

Over the next few months my arms began to strengthen and I could move them more freely. I had regained significant improvement in my motor functions; which are the transmissions of messages from the brain to muscle groups to create movement. I had progressed from forty days of no movement to the return of motor function in my shoulders and biceps. To this day, that's all the function the good Lord would provide me. However, it was enough to give me hope. With movement in my shoulders and biceps, I was eventually able to feed myself, type, write, control my electric wheelchair and most importantly hug my loved ones. It restored a piece of my confidence that was presumed lost four months ago in the ocean.

One day a nurse came in to feed me and insisted I eat lunch sitting up. I explained my routine, but she continued to try to get me to open my mouth. The more she insisted, the more I yelled "No." She was a stubborn Irish lass that wouldn't stop pestering me. After about ten minutes of back and forth hassling I got my arms underneath the plate and let it fly, splattering meatballs and pasta all over her uniform. Understandably, she shouted a few expletives and ran out the door crying. It was the last time she would enter my room. The head nurse came to check out the commotion and walked away laughing. One of the aides kindly went across the street to grab me a sandwich from the local deli. To this day, I will bark loudly when pushed into a corner.

By mid-October I received permission to go home for the weekend. The objective was to allow loved ones to learn what to expect when I was finally discharged. My dad would pick me up Saturday morning and we'd return Sunday night. Within an hour of arriving home my friends would start to show up for a visit. There were over twenty the first time and every week after, fewer and fewer would stop by. When one has a traumatic event you quickly learn who your real friends are. We're only human.

Visits always started with the usual comments such as "How are you doing and you're looking good." After the pleasantries faded, my friends would talk among themselves about school events and other events going on at that time. Since I was clueless what they were chatting about, I was left feeling very uncomfortable. I had become a ghost and the proverbial *lamp shade* at my own party. Driving back to rehab that Sunday night I realized I was caught in God's version of purgatory: trapped between my old life and trying to figure out what my new life had in store.

In November, my classmates threw a fund raiser for me with a students versus teachers basketball game. The week leading up to the event I went for my monthly x-ray to determine if the full body cast was still necessary. My hopes were fixated on positive news. However, Dr. Petrillo said let's give it another month. Ouch that hurt. Now that I understood that I'd have to wear the cast to the game, my knees were already shaking.

When that dreadful night was upon me, I felt something that I had never experienced entering the high school before. They have many names for it, nervousness, the shakes, but basically I was scared *shitless*. Once I arrived and was lifted into my wheelchair, one of my friends pushed me to the gym. As we got close to the door, I could see the gym was packed. When my friends and the rest of the crowd saw me, they started chanting my nickname, "Gules, Gules, Gules." This reception gave me the goose bumps and brought me to the verge of tears. After a few minutes, I said a few words to the crowd, while secretly praying that the game would start quickly. I would have had a much better time without the cast, but I survived. What doesn't kill us makes us stronger.

The following weekend on my visit home, my dad accidentally placed the cast by the oven and the heat melted much of it. It is a shame it hadn't happened the prior week. That Monday, rather than remolding the cast, Dr. Petrillo decided I didn't need it anymore. He had me use just a hard collar instead. Thank God for unintended consequences.

The Monday through Friday routine was becoming a grind and weekends couldn't come soon enough. One Tuesday night I received a call from Mike, my dad's lifelong friend. He asked if I would like to go out for dinner. I replied absolutely. Since one of my rehab roommates, Larry, from Florida, rarely had visitors, I asked Mike if he could join us. He said as long as we had permission from the head nurse. Thankfully, she granted it.

Dinner was going to be at Limericks, a steak house restaurant two city blocks away. This was our first outing and proved to be a challenge for Mike. He had to push me half a block and then apply my brakes, then go back and get Larry and repeated the process. Mike proceeded back and forth three more times before we all reached the entrance to Limericks only to discover there was a large step to get inside. Mike went inside, rounded up some strong guys who carried us in our wheelchairs. We were inside in a blink of the eye. The food was delicious and we all enjoyed the evening. Mike got us back safely, said goodnight, and off into the dark he went, probably exhausted.

The following weekend couldn't come fast enough. It would be the first time I'd go out alone with just my friends. My closest friend Joseph, a classmate and I were going out to the movies to see *American Graffiti*. For the first six years after my injury, anytime I would go out with my friends, it was necessary for them to lift me out of the chair and place me in the passenger seat. Thank God, all my friends were in good shape and strong. Obviously, the first time was a learning curve for all of us and created a few awkward moments. On this occasion, Joseph lifted me like a feather, placed me in the front seat and buckled me up. As soon as he parked at the theater, he and my classmate jumped out of the car and started heading toward the theater only to realize that they had forgotten me. Smoothly back tracking wasn't enough to save him from embarrassment. Somehow Joseph locked me and the keys inside the car. Now what? Since I was unable to reach the lock, he had to jimmy the door open with a coat hanger. We couldn't stop laughing as we went inside the theater. It was a breath of fresh air being out in the public again, enjoying things that one usually takes for granted.

The next weekend, we were going to Hofstra University to watch my high school basketball team play Roslyn for the county championship. Our team was far superior to Roslyn's and we were looking for a good game. I thought this would be an ideal time to return coach Mintz's chain and charm. After Joseph placed it in an envelope and stuck it between my fingers, he rolled me toward the coach. I reached toward him and handed it back. He wasn't sure what was inside. Once he gazed into the envelope his eyes got watery. We hugged and went back to our sitting area. Coach then called the team off the court and back to the locker room. I'm not a hundred percent sure but I believe he explained what transpired and used this to inspire the team. From tip-off to the final buzzer the team had a miserable game....season over. So much for the rally cry, "Win one for the Gipper."

Two weeks later I was discharged from rehab and was heading home.

Chapter 11 - Back home

Leaving the rehab center after nine months was bitter-sweet. The staff had become my extended family with many solid friendships established. My parents now had the burden of caring for me around the clock. This made me a bit apprehensive and filled me with a whole lot of guilt. My parents should have been preparing for their golden years, not taking care of me.

Now that I was home, it became quite apparent the devastating effect that my accident had cast on the family. My dad was stoical. He was able to distract himself from thinking about me by going to work each day. He had his emotional outlet. Mom wasn't so lucky. She was reminded of what happened to her baby boy twenty-four hours a day. She grasped all her inner strength to suppress her feelings. Her tears went unseen; her cries unheard. The eyes are said to be the window to the soul. Looking at my mom her soul was shattered. Intuition tells me not a day went by when my mom wouldn't question God's decision. Why not me instead of my child, I'm certain is what she thought. Wouldn't any loving and nurturing mother contemplate the same thoughts? There is a saying, "Time heals all wounds". That is a fallacy when it comes to a mom's anguish when one of her children is harmed. Once a shining light in her life, I now felt like a dark cloud. This left me wondering. Would the family have been better off if God had snatched me away while I was floating head down in the ocean that fateful day?

My family and I thought we were prepared for my return home but we had a steep adjustment period in front of us. When things ran as smoothly as a well-oiled machine life was enjoyable. When things went astray, life was miserable. Schedules had to be adjusted around me because it took two to transfer me from the bed to the wheelchair. Mom's job was to get me dressed. My dad or my sister would come home during their lunch break to assist the transfer. It really sucked!

In the rehabilitation center there was always help at your fingertips. The regiment kept me so occupied, leaving no time to grasp the ripple effect of a spinal cord injury. They would dress me, not my mother. The humiliation of this is not meant to be endured, especially as a teenager. For the first time since the accident, the feelings of independence, freedom and privacy were lost. I was imprisoned in a wheelchair for life. The worst sentence God could dish out. No parole, no pardon, and no time off for good behavior.

While in rehab my parents bought a ranch style house on the other side of Syosset. The ranch was roughly a thousand yards from the high school which made it convenient for me. There was no way I could have stayed in the split level with all those stairs. Reluctantly, I slowly adjusted to the change in venue.

The remainder of the school year a tutor came to the house so

I could receive credit for the year. I passed. The summer was now upon us.

Chapter 12 - Main Streaming

School would be starting the day after Labor Day which always falls on the first Monday in September. Like most things in my life, at this time, nothing went as smoothly as expected and returning to school would be no exception.

It was early August when we received a letter from the Superintendent of Syosset School District. He wanted to meet with us to discuss my needs for the upcoming school year. The letter also contained a date, time and location for this meeting.

As we entered into the conference room we were surprised to see so many people. The Superintendent, the entire school board and other members of the administration were in attendance. Immediately I knew this wasn't going to be a slam dunk.

The Superintendent started the meeting by welcoming us and introducing himself and the school board. Then the real fireworks started when he said that after reviewing my case with the school board they came to consensus that it would be in my best interest to be home tutored for my senior year. The school would provide everything necessary to succeed. He went on to say it was for my safety and that of my classmates.

My family and I were stunned for a few seconds, but then the alpha dog, Dad, jumped to his feet. My dad was President of the Machinist Union. Standing up for individual's rights was his forte. He slammed the desk and pointed directly at the Superintendent. Raising his intimidating voice, so all could hear, my dad said, "Come hell or high water, my son is going to attend this high school with his classmates." He continued, "Rob will be on the school's doorstep come first day of school. If the district refused him entrance, every elected town official, every news agency would be alerted. If need be, a local lawyer would be hired to fight this in court."

Everyone in the room was in shock. The dumbfounded Superintendent asked if we wouldn't mind stepping out of the room so he could talk to the school board.

Ten minutes passed. Then, we were summoned back to the conference room. The Superintendent admitted that he had underestimated our determination to return to school. He went on to say I could return based on two conditions. First, I had to agree to be bused to and from school. Second, I had to report to the nurse's office as soon as I arrived on campus. We quickly agreed to the terms. I said thank you, but what I really wanted to tell them was that they were overpaid *stuff-shirts* who should be ashamed of themselves. Then we marched out with big smiles on our faces.

Remember it was 1974 and many college campuses were protesting the Vietnam war, having walkouts and sit-ins to get their message heard. To this day, I wonder if my classmates would have walked out if I had been denied entrance.

While the question remains unanswered, my heart believes they would have done the right thing.

Chapter 13 - Senior Year

The first day of school had finally arrived and it was the complete opposite feeling that I had entering tenth grade. The confidence, excitement and mojo that once embraced me had long faded away. I was nervous and scared of everything, a mere shadow of how most remembered me. *How will my classmates and teachers accept me now, wheelchair and all?*

An aftereffect of having a spinal cord injury can be involuntary muscles spasms. From time to time my leg would tighten up and begin bouncing up and down. I was on a muscle relaxing medication which did little for the spasms. Instead, it mellowed me into a zombie. The muscle spasms were annoying to me because it gave everyone around me the impression I was going to have a seizure. I couldn't blame them because that's exactly how it looked.

On that first day, the bus drove up our driveway as agreed upon exactly at eight. The driver leapt out, came up to the door and introduced himself. He then proceeded to push me to the bus and onto the hydraulic lift. Once situated in the bus he strapped the wheelchair down and buckled my seatbelts. Two minutes later we were at the front entrance of the school and out of the bus I came. This process would be repeated in the afternoon. I wish I could tell you that I abided by the agreed terms with the school district, but on some sunny days a friend would push me home.

Greeting me at the school door were Charles and Lisa. Charles was Joseph's younger brother and in eleventh grade. He was a good-hearted friend whom I have known since we were six and five respectively. Lisa was a fellow senior who I got to know in junior high and was the kind of person that would give you the shirt off her back. They both welcomed me back and then strolled with me to the nursing station to sign in. Looking back, I laugh because not one member of the administration was there to welcome me.

My curriculum for the year was English vocabulary, math, cinema arts and accounting. The first class started at eight thirty and my last class finished by noon. Notes were provided by my classmates and tests were given orally by the teacher. Either I knew the answer or I didn't. No smooth talking could rescue me.

Sure enough, during my first class a spasm occurred. Everyone turned around to see what was happening. There wasn't a big enough rock for me to hide underneath. I was off to a flying start. One of my classmates was kind enough to place my foot back on the pedal rest. This young lady's gesture put my stress level at ease. Over time, things greatly improved and we all adjusted to the new me.

The school year went by like a blur. Everyone seemed to be moving at warp speed while I was going in slow motion. Most of my classmates had already been accepted to their chosen college or university while I was playing catchup. Missing my entire junior year really set me back. Now it was time to figure out my future. I scheduled a meeting with my guidance counselor.

During our first meeting I mentioned my interest in majoring in accounting. The counselor asked for a week so he could do his research and penciled me in for the following week. When I returned he had literature and catalogs for the schools he was recommending. They were, Wayne State in the middle of Detroit, University of Buffalo where winters and winds are brutal, and the University of South Florida. He must not have been very fond of me. The family did take a trip to check out USF. It had a beautiful campus, but I wasn't ready to be away from home and dependent on strangers. I left school not knowing where I was going to attend. The only thing I knew was that college had to be somewhere close to home.

Graduation day was a very special event. Ceremonies were held on the football field. The stage and the podium were located on the visitor's sidelines, folding chairs in rows of twenty five were aligned on the field, and the parents and guests sat in the home team bleachers. I was encouraged to arrive a few minutes early to get situated on the far left of the first row. Within minutes the bleachers were packed and all the dignitaries situated on the stage. Our senior class was composed of nearly seven hundred students. Two by two, they marched to their assigned seats. After the dignitaries and class valedictorian delivered their speeches, it was time to receive our diplomas. Unbeknownst to me, my name was to be called first. As my friend started pushing me up the make shift ramp to the platform to receive my diploma, I noticed a few classmates standing and clapping. Once settled on the stage, I looked out at a sea of red caps and gowns. Not only the entire class, but everyone in the bleachers and on the stage, was giving me a standing ovation. It lasted a couple of minutes. The outpouring of love, admiration, and appreciation for my reaching this milestone caught me totally off guard. It was a heart stopping moment that rocked my world. For the first time since the accident, I fully realized how much others appreciated my strength and fortitude in achieving this milestone. Against all odds, I had graduated with my class. This felt fantastic.

Chapter 14 – Higher Education

Prior to my first semester of college I accepted a summer job at Jones Beach, one mile south of Tobay Beach, the place that forever changed my life. The irony was not lost on me. My job entailed checking security bands which allowed access to the locker rooms. Every morning, my sister, Sue, drove me. She had to lift me out of the wheelchair into her Toyota Corolla and then off we'd go. The first year, my hours were nine to three. Susan would hang out for the six hours at the beach and then drive me home. How many sisters would do this for their brother? She was a physical education teacher and had summers off. As luck would have it, a month passed before a manager approached Susan and asked her if she would like a job. She gladly accepted the position.

My sister turned that opportunity into a lifelong career. When Susan recently retired, she was the first woman to hold the position of Director of NY State Parks on Long Island. See what a good brother she has. Sometimes, good things happen to good people. There is no better person than my sister and I am so proud of her accomplishments.

Her main concentration was on Jones Beach Park and she was

given a rent free four bedroom house on the park's property. Jones Beach State Park, beside the beach and a five mile boardwalk, is home to a twelve thousand seat amphitheater that hosts musical concerts from major performing artists throughout the summer season. Over the years we have seen the likes of Phil Collins, Tina Turner, The Who, Fleetwood Mac, and Jimmy Buffet to name a few. Nydia, who you'll meet later, and I would plan our long weekend getaways based on the concert schedule.

There was a police barracks next to my sister's house. When Jimmy Buffet performed there, he would helicopter in and land on their front lawn. On one occasion, Nydia and I went out to greet him. He was the easiest going, laid back superstar one could meet. We chattered for a good five minutes and took pictures. There are few things more entertaining than going to a Buffet concert in an open air venue surrounded by 12,000 wild *parrot heads*. The following year, we would greet him again. He remembered our encounter the previous summer. It was humbling considering how many people he must meet over the course of a year. He is a classy guy.

Fall semester was rapidly approaching and I was still pondering what college to attend. Living on campus was already ruled out which narrowed my search to a handful of schools. I decided on the C.W. Post campus, affiliated with Long Island University, and chose accounting as my major. Due to my late application I had to meet with the Dean of Accounting before they would accept me. Fortunately, the Dean said welcome aboard and then put me on probation for the first semester. There was never the easy way for me. There were two overriding factors in school selection. Both my best friend, Joseph, and my girlfriend, Lisa, were in attendance there.

Joseph and I have been the best of friends our entire life. There is something special about a childhood friendship. It's sacred. Think about how many people come and go in our lives. If you're lucky enough to have a friendship that lasts a lifetime, thank the good Lord. I am even more blessed to have that relationship with him. A true friend is someone that has touched your heart, someone that you mutually care for unconditionally. We have that in spades.

He is a brother to me and has always had my back. While others scattered, he was always there. Our friendship has spanned over fifty years and to this day it is as strong as ever. When I asked Joseph if he would be willing to drive me to and from school he slapped me on the back of the head, quickly replied of course, and then lectured me on the stupid nature of the question. Since Joseph was a business major, we arranged our class schedules for the same time. After working out the kinks the first week, we were as smooth as Butch Cassidy and the Sundance Kid. He would lift me out of the chair and drop me into his Camaro's bucket seat. Then he would fold the wheelchair and throw it in the trunk. Monday, Wednesday, Friday our classes were from nine to twelve. Tuesday and Thursday we were in class from nine to eleven. The State of NY Vocational Rehabilitation paid for my tuition and books throughout college. I made sure that my buddy got compensated from the state for his assistance. Joseph was reluctant to accept the stipend because he wasn't helping me for the money. After I convinced him to accept it, we agreed to use the money for good times. That's his character. It makes me proud to call Joseph my brother and I am blessed he is in my life.

Lisa and I dated for three years. She was attracted to me since ninth grade and we began dating in our senior year of high school. My being in a wheelchair did not intimidate her. She was devoted to my well-being and was far too caring for the lost puppy I was. Unfortunately, we had a love/hate relationship. My immaturity and insecurities were the cause. Even though we had many good times, I cheated her out of so many more. One opportunity for a good time that I vividly recall ruining was the senior prom. Every senior looks forward to that evening and Lisa was no different. She pleaded with me to go and I refused. The thought of attending seemed like more trouble than it was worth. She didn't want to go alone so we watched the Yankees game that evening. The real truth, I was scared of being around so many classmates.

Even though Joseph wasn't very fond of Lisa, he appreciated how well she took care of me. This uneasiness left me in an awkward situation. When Joseph was around Lisa became an afterthought. When he wasn't, I cuddled up to her. The word *used* can be harsh, but at times it applied to my behavior toward her. No one should every treat another person that way. Yet, I did. Just recently I found the courage to apologize to her for my actions which she gracefully accepted.

The first semester I made the Dean's list which made everyone elated and got me off probation. Going into my second year my schedule included three difficult accounting classes. On the first day we realized the classes were being held on the second floor in a building with no elevator. It took the school six weeks to finally relocate the classes to an accessible facility. That screw up made it impossible for me to catch up causing me to change my major to business administration. Between this incident and missing a semester for medical reasons it took me five years, rather than four, to graduate. The change in majors didn't bother me. I just wanted the diploma and the satisfaction of completing something that many fail to do.

Studying, writing term papers and taking tests proved to be challenging. It took the help of friends, family, classmates and my God-given intelligence. Joseph and Lisa would move me from class to class. On the first day of every new class, I would scout out who appeared to be the smartest and the best note taker. I would then inquire if that person would be willing to provide a copy. Everyone enjoyed assisting me. I never missed a class and always sat in the first row. I wear wrist splints, similar to those worn by sufferers of carpal tunnel, to keep my hands from flopping. A cuff is attached to hold a pencil in place. With the eraser portion I'm able to turn pages. When a fork is attached to this cuff I can feed myself. Laptops would have come in handy, but this was still the age of the typewriter. My term papers had to be dictated to my mom, who would then type them. I'd wake up at two in the morning and would still hear the clicking of keystrokes from the typewriter. It made me feel guilty as hell, but she never complained. She also deserved a special diploma with all the hours spent. What a mom. Tests were given orally by the professor or their assistant, others taken in the hallway with a proctor, and if I got lucky some trusted me to complete the work at home. This system worked for me and I have the sheep skin to verify it.

Obstacles, especially steps, were a rampant problem to those in wheelchairs in the seventies and eighties. It wasn't until 1990, when the Americans with Disabilities Act (ADA) was signed, that all public places were compelled to be wheelchair accessible. Single steps, most of the time were a non-factor for me because the person accompanying me was strong enough to pop a wheelie and place the two front wheels on the top step. Then, all he had to do was lift the back of the wheelchair until the back wheels were also on the step. Multiple steps, on the other hand, proved impossible.

To me, the extra year just wasn't the same since Joseph had graduated and Lisa had transferred to a state school. They were both gone. Fortunately, Joseph's younger brother, Charles, volunteered to be wheel-man for my final year. I now had a new modified van with a lift, and I attended classes at night. In order to graduate, I was required to pass a computer programming class. On two other occasions I was forced to drop this class. Was the third time going to be the charm? For some reason the logic of programming was difficult to grasp and I barely got by with a *D*. Walking off the campus on that final day, when Charles asked me what I wanted to do with that computer book, I replied, "Throw it away." We laughed. My computer days were over.

I graduated in May of 1980 with a Bachelor's of Science degree in Business Administration and a B average. It wasn't an easy ride but having that diploma in my hands proved I could accomplish great things even in a wheelchair. Looking back at my college days one thought continues to puzzle me. Over the five years at school I did not make a single friend that left an impression on me. Maybe because I was surrounded by my inner circle, possibly because we commuted, or maybe it was just shyness. Whatever the reason, life went on.

That summer my uncle arranged an interview for me in the IBM office located in Queens. Uncle Jack had clout at IBM and most of his children were already on their payroll. The office was a thirty minute drive on the Long Island Expressway (L.I.E) during off-peak hours. During rush hour, it became ninety minutes of bumper to bumper agony. At the interview, I was told that the position entailed being a dispatcher. This meant that family members wanting to get in touch with their love ones would call me first. I, in turn, would know where in the field they were and then relay the message. Remember, cell phones weren't invented yet. It was a good entry level position at one of the world's largest companies. Of course, I turned it down. The ninety minutes commute each way would have put too much stress on my body. Furthermore, I was purely delusional. I had this notion that after college one should start as a manager with a staff. Hey, I now know that I was stupid and naive, but it didn't take me long to face reality.

In order to keep my parents off my back I decided to start graduate school by attending Adelphi University for one semester. After performing poorly on the GMAT's (graduate school entrance exams) the school reluctantly admitted me. The funny thing is they didn't hesitate to cash my seven hundred dollar check. And that was just for one class. I started by taking a micro economics class which was exactly the same class I took in undergraduate school. Since I already mastered that class, instead of studying, I would spend the afternoon in the backyard getting a suntan while listening to my radio rock. After dinner, I was off to class wearing my dungarees, T-shirt, sneakers and sunglasses. I'd arrive early and watch my classmates trickle in. They all had professional jobs and wore three piece suits or dresses. They were there for one reason while I was there to hide out. During the semester I took a two week vacation to Florida with the family. Bringing the economics book on the trip to study was a joke. It never came out of the van. When the final came, I discovered that I was clueless. The professor gave me a D. That was the end my formal education.

Chapter 15 – Trial Time

A few days following my injury, an attorney friend of my dad's gave him a call. He wanted to inquire on my status and to ask if there was anything he could do to help out. My dad knew him from the church and they bowled together in a league. He strongly recommended that my dad file a lawsuit against the Town of Oyster Bay, the operators of the beach. My dad told him he had no time for a lawsuit since all his efforts were devoted to keeping me alive. The lawyer responded that he would handle everything and all he needed was permission to pursue. Dad said do what you think is best and left it at that.

We had never given the lawsuit a single thought until about a year after being discharged from Rusk Institute when we received a letter from the lawyers representing the town. They wanted to set a time and date to meet and depose me. My dad called them and arranged everything. The deposition was to take place in our living room where our lawyer, the town lawyer, a stenographer and myself gathered. After being sworn in, the meeting lasted about an hour. The majority of questions concerned my recollection, to the best of my knowledge, of all the events that occurred on that dreaded day. Another two years elapsed before we received any news regarding the case. This time the town insisted that I go for a medical examination at their appointed hospital and medical staff. They must have thought I was faking this whole nightmare in order to collect a few bucks. One look at me and five minutes of questioning was all the doctor needed to know. The doctor apologized for wasting our time and wished us good luck.

Again, a few more years passed before we would hear more about the case. Our lawyer's assistant called to inform us that our case was on the court's docket. I was in shock. We were finally going to trial.

To an outsider, my accident was an act of God and the fault of mother nature, which made no one culpable, not even me. In all honesty this thought had crossed my mind many times. But our grievance wasn't against nature itself but rather mankind's disturbance of it. We learned prior to the summer season, it was common practice for the local towns to hire the Army Corps of Engineers to bulldoze all the sand that eroded onto the beach back into the ocean. Doing this can cause the buildup of sandbars close to shore and unnoticeable to the naked eye. Since, no other objects or warning signs were located in the area of my accident, we claimed it was a hidden sandbar that I struck.

Given the complexity of this case, my dad's friend, who was a town attorney, realized this case required a litigation specialist. So, he referred me to a big time NYC lawyer by the name of Judge Finz. Finz was a retired judge who had returned to private practice and was now totally devoted to litigation law. Trust me, he was the kind of lawyer you see on all the television shows and then some.

Finz was in his early fifties and sharp as a tack. He wore five hundred dollar suits, drove a Bentley and smoked Cuban cigars. The minute he walked into our home I knew if we were going to win or lose this case I would be in the hands of the best. The courtroom was his stage and he was the maestro.

We met with Finz and his two assistants a couple of days prior to the start of the trial to go over my story and get our instructions. He told us how to dress, where to sit in the courtroom, how to behave, who to look at, and what facial expressions to display. His last parting words were, "Lets kick some ass now." We all chuckled. He was confident his clients were ready.

Walking into the court room gave me goose bumps. I immediately spotted Finz and his team getting organized at their table. He gave me a quick wink and went back to making his final preparations. The town lawyer was doing the same at his table. He was a tall slender man, with jet black hair, well-dressed and in his late thirties. When both lawyers were ready the judge walked in and the bailiff shouted, "All rise." The judge sat and then everyone followed his lead. The judge called the court in session, introduced himself and went over his ground rules. He then turned to the bailiff and ordered him to bring in the jurors, all twelve of them.

The lawyers on both sides made their opening statements and convincingly presented their sides of the case. I realized this wasn't going to be an easy case. But then again, after my accident nothing had come easy so why should this be any different. When the judge gave Finz the green light to start, he called his first witness, a town administrator in charge of beach operations. Finz bombarded him with questions and comments that made him look foolish. By the time he finished his questioning the poor man had aged ten years. Next up was the town employee who was in charge of on-site day to day business at the beach. Finz stood up and continued where he left off, grilling him relentlessly and showing no mercy. This witness was even more uninformed than his boss. When the witness stepped down the judge gave some parting instructions and adjourned for the day. On the way home, my mom said she felt sorry for what the two witnesses had endured.

That night, before falling asleep, I replayed the events of that day and tried to determine which way I would be leaning if I were on the jury. Trying to remove my bias in the decision, I decided that the verdict was too close to call with a slight edge to team Finz. Every night this pattern would continue until the outcome was determined.

Day two proceeded as the day before. One by one, Finz embarrassed everyone associated with the oversight of the beach restoration and demonstrated their incompetence. After we adjourned for the day, Finz went back to our house where he met with our expert oceanographer to prepare him for tomorrow's questions and proper answers. A good lawyer never asks a question without knowing the response. The two men went into a spare bedroom and began rehearsing. No more than five minutes passed before everyone heard Finz screaming at our expert witness, "If you're not going to be a team player then get the hell out of here." We never saw the oceanographer again.

As each day proceeded, my anxiety level rose. Soon or later I was going to be called to testify. My turn was approaching quickly. On the third day, Finz called to the witness stand one of the teenage girls who had accompanied me to the beach that day. After he finished his line of questioning, it was the defense's turn to cross-examine the witness. Each question the lawyer asked Finz objected to and each time the judge overruled him. This went on for ten minutes before Finz told the judge his rulings were wrong. The judge took exception to Finz's comments and told him to show him a brief* proving his objections were correct. Finz opened the inside of his suit jacket as he glared right at the judge and said, "I don't carry them on me." The judge adjourned early that day due to other scheduling conflicts. A brief is:

a written legal argument, usually in a format prescribed by the courts, stating the legal reasons for the suit based on statutes, regulations, case precedents, legal texts, and reasoning applied to facts in the particular situation. A brief is submitted to lay out the argument for various petitions and motions before the court (sometimes called "points and authorities"), to counter the arguments of opposing lawyers, and to provide the judge or judges with reasons to rule in favor of the party represented by the brief writer. Occasionally on minor or follow-up legal issues, the judge will specify that a letter or memorandum brief will be sufficient. On appeals and certain other major arguments, the brief is bound with color-coded covers stipulated in state and/or federal court rules. Ironically, although the term was originally intended to mean a brief or summary argument (shorter than an oral presentation), legal briefs are quite often notoriously long.

On day four, I instantly noticed numerous law books on my lawyer's table all with bookmarks sticking out of them. Once the judge entered and the jurors were seated Finz asked if he could approach the bench. Both lawyers stood together facing the judge and began whispering back and forth. The judge then directed the bailiff to return the jurors back to their conference room and then asked the lawyers to join him in his chambers. We had no clue what was happening, but all the books were carried into chambers by Finz's assistants. My family all looked at each other and shrugged our shoulders wondering what we should do. It didn't take long before everyone but the jurors returned. The now red-faced judge informed us that Finz's objections were valid. He then said that he would declare a mistrial unless the two sides could decide on an acceptable monetary settlement. He then added that we had four hours to reach that agreement before bolting into his chambers.

Determining an appropriate amount is like playing Russian roulette. You want to get as much money as possible and avoid going for a new trial. The town approached with an initial offer which we all agreed was unacceptable. My dad proposed a counter offer which the town refused. The next offer by the town was reasonable and Finz asked me what I thought. I looked him in the eye and said you're the professional what do you think. Finz thought it was fair. He explained to us that pushing any further could be treacherous. Since the settlement was enough to provide me with a good income stream, we accepted. Part of the settlement agreement forbade me from disclosingthe actual monetary amount. However, I will tell you that it was a fair settlement.

After all the papers were signed, we said our thanks and farewells. Judge Finz kissed me on the forehead, wished me luck and told me to invest the money conservatively. It was easy to invest in 1982. Interest rates on bank CD's and US Treasuries were twelve percent. Even the town lawyer was happy that we had settled and wished us nothing but the best. Exiting the court house, we were stopped by two jurors who told us that they had been pulling for us and had hoped that we received some compensation. I gave them a quick nod yes and thanked them for their support.

No money is worth the pain and anguish resulting from my accident but the settlement sure was a major step in my goal for independence. With my two diplomas and money in the bank, the pieces of the puzzle of my new life were starting materialize.

Chapter 16 – Lift Inc.

Less than two months after the trial I received a call from Michelle, my vocational rehabilitation counselor. The sole purpose of the vocational rehabilitation counselor was to provide physically and/or mentally challenged individuals with the resources and tools necessary to learn a skill so they could enter the work force and become a productive member of society. Michelle was excellent at her job and was extremely generous to me. She got the state funded agency to pay my entire undergraduate education, provide me with a new electric wheelchair and retrofit my van with a hydraulic lift.

Michelle called to discuss a job training opportunity that was being sponsored by a non-profit organization called Lift Incorporated. Lift matched disabled people with a Fortune 500 company where they could learn how to code the programs that ran the mainframe computer. One day a week I would be expected to go to the company for formal training, the other four were spent self-teaching via video tapes and manuals. Access to a mainframe terminal would be installed at my house with connectivity to the company's systems. This was before the birth of PCs and the internet. Upon successful completion of the program the partnering company guaranteed a three month job with the hopes of turning it into a full time career. Having no better options at the time, I agreed to give it a try. Michelle concluded by wishing me good luck and told me I'd be hearing from a Lift coordinator soon.

Five minutes later, Linda, the Lift coordinator, called to arrange an interview and an aptitude test. We met the following Monday to discuss the program, take the aptitude test and answer any questions or concerns we both may have had. Linda didn't portray any warmth, strictly business. She said her intentions were to pair me with MetLife Insurance and she would be arranging for me to meet with their managers. I said fine.

The meeting with the MetLife managers went smoothly. It is amazing how much confidence one can display when they have a few dollars in the bank. Throughout the entire meeting all I could think of was they needed me more than I need them.

When the training period concluded I was assigned to a MetLife satellite office out in Hauppauge. The office was located thirty miles further east on the Island from my house. This was advantageous because I would always be traveling in the opposite direction of the rush hour crowd. I only went to the office once a week for three hours. The rest of the time they assumed I was working diligently at home. Guess again.

My supervisor was a wimpish nerd who gave me my first assignment. MetLife sold medical policies to large blue chip companies. I was hired to rewrite a poorly written program for General Motors. It consisted of eight hundred lines of code that he wanted me to cut in half.

With my assignment completed and the three month trial period over it was up to my supervisor whether or not to hire me on a full time basis. He had never said a word to me in the past three months and elected not to offer me a position. My co-workers were surprised by his decision, but it rolled right off my back.

Within an hour of arriving home the phone was ringing off the hook. It was Linda expressing her disbelief in my supervisor's decision. She informed me that his manager wanted to bring me back under the lead of a different supervisor. So what did I do? I asked for a raise. I wish I had done it face to face because I'm certain that she peed on herself. After her begging MetLife to give me a second chance, going back to them again with a request for more money would only make her sound crazy. I responded, "No raise, no work". She slammed the phone down in disgust. Ten minutes later the phone rang again. I got my raise.

When I went in to greet my new supervisor, the manager was also present. We chatted for a few moments then the supervisor gave me my new assignment and showed me to my cubicle. I stared at the monitor for a couple minutes, then backed out of the cubicle and knocked on the manager's office door. I had no interest in this type of work at this stage in my life and felt he should know that. We spent two hours talking about everything but the job. He understood my decision and wished me good luck. He went on to say if I ever changed my mind he would welcome me back. I couldn't have asked for a cooler, more sincere man, and I appreciated what he said.

After departing MetLife, I realized the time spent during the training and hands on experience wasn't a total waste of my time. Besides the monetary compensation, I had learned how to work in a corporate environment and had developed computer skills that could be used in the future.

Most people would have called Linda immediately to explain what had just transpired, but not me. I waited for her to call me and listened to her go ballistic. She didn't disappoint me and after a few minutes I told her thank you for the opportunity, goodbye and hung up. My handling of the situation wasn't very professional. But live and learn. Besides finding the work tedious there was another reason I had decided to leave.

I had a medical issue that warranted surgery and three months of healing. Rather than explaining this to everyone, including Linda, and expecting them to keep my position open, I bowed out gracefully.

There are three major medical nemesis that haunt victims of spinal cord injuries. They are lung infections, urinary tract infections and pressure sores. My Achilles heel has always been a reoccurring pressure sore on my left buttock.

Have you ever sat for a long period of a time and then stood up because your butt hurt? That pain you feel is the blood vessels being choked off killing the buttock muscle and telling you to get off your ass. Unfortunately, not feeling that pain and sitting long hours catches up to me. Once that occurs it's surgery and a lengthy recovery. Ugh!

Chapter 17 – Miss Nydia

It was early January in 1985 when my dad and I drove into Manhattan to have my surgery at NYU Medical Center. The surgery was called a muscular rotational flap of the left buttocks muscle to cover the pressure sore. The plastic surgeon is able to rotate the damaged section to a non-pressure area and replace it with fresh healthy muscle. Thus covering the hole. This is followed by the dreaded eight weeks of bed rest, before I can begin to sit again. Sitting is limited to thirty minutes. Over the next few weeks, pending no setbacks, sitting time is increased by fifteen minute intervals.

Prior to leaving the house I told my friend, Brian Landau, I wasn't coming home alone this time. He chuckled in doubt, as my dad strapped the wheelchair down in the van and I yelled back, "You'll see." I was turning twenty-eight in April. It was time to get serious about settling down and what better place to meet lovely ladies than the hospital.

Brian and I met a few years earlier. He was working for a health agency and was assigned my case for two hours a day. Brian had graduated college with a degree in business before realizing it wasn't the career he was looking for. His calling was to help those struggling to find their way in life. Besides working for me, he was a counselor at a boy's home. The first day he showed up in a white shirt and dress slacks. Immediately, I told him no more uniforms. Casual clothes were fine. He smiled at that. Having never worked with a paralyzed individual, he was intimidated and nervous. His responsibilities were to help transfer me in the wheelchair, assist with lunch, and any remaining time we play games of backgammon. Within a few weeks he was a member of the family and arrived at the house on his Harley motorcycle, dressed in blue jeans, tee shirt, leather jacket and black boots. Brian was now at ease.

I arrived on the eleventh floor to be admitted. The office clerk directed me to room seven and informed me that the nurse would be in shortly. When Nydia walked in we were all smiles and gave each other a warm embrace. We had met during my previous hospital stays, and I had secretly liked her. Nydia was a gorgeous woman, roughly five foot three, weighed one hundred and twenty pounds, brown hair and eyes. On top of that, she was a fantastic nurse. Born in Puerto Rico, she had moved to New York at age eight. She came to America with the burning desire to help others. She quickly learned English. In high school, she volunteered as a candy striper at a local hospital. From there she was trained as a nurse's aide. Always wanting to better herself, she continued her education and obtained her degree in nursing, becoming an RN. We had many pleasant conversations and she provided me with excellent care over the years. I was elated she was assigned to take care of me once again. While she was drilling me with questions to complete the admitting forms I noticed that a wedding ring was absent from her hand. Could this be the one?

Nydia is always in constant motion. She is a perfectionist and a true hands-on registered nurse. In today's world, nurses sit behind a desk in front of computer screens while the nurse's aides do all the grunt work. After completing the paperwork, Nydia took all my vitals and put me in bed. My dad helped her get me undressed so they could get a closer look at the wound. After Nydia lectured me for allowing this to happen, she left for the day.

Bright and early the next day Nydia came in to give me my morning medications and to prep me for surgery. Surgery was set for noon. I was all washed up and ready to go when the transport team arrived with the gurney. Nydia wished me good luck and said she'll be off tomorrow but would be back the following day. That evening one of the nurses informed me that Nydia had just called to check on my status. I slept with a big smile that night. Her interest in me went above and beyond.

Surgery was the easy part; the recuperation was the torture. My arm agility is greatly compromised when I lie in bed, due to gravity, and it leaves me unable to do anything for myself. All the conditions for a terrible experience are compounded by the fact that the majority of my time is spent lying on my stomach. This torture would last for eight weeks before I would eventually be able to slowly sit up again. Ugh!

I spent eleven days in the hospital before moving down to the rehabilitation center. Nydia took care of me nine of those days, but she was off the day I was transferred. Questions such as why they couldn't wait one more day and would I ever see Nydia again raced through my head. All my questions and concerns would be answered the next day.

My rehabilitation doctor thought it would be refreshing for me if I got out of the room once a day. He had the staff hoist me onto a gurney and parked me in that hallway. Still lying on my stomach, I quickly learned to identify those walking past me by their shoes. One by one, the staff walked by until I saw a small pair of white shoes stop right in front of me. Yes, those were Nydia's feet and my doubts were wiped away. My Cinderella had appeared and my heart felt the flames of desire.

From that time on, she would stop by each day during lunch and eventually we would eat dinner together. Every minute we spent together filled my heart with love. The unknown question was did she feel the same way toward me? I knew it was now time for me to make the dreaded first move. The fear of rejection had reared its ugly head and I knew it could be slayed. With my courage in my throat, I asked if it would be ok to kiss her. Her response would weaken any man. "What took you so long?" she said. A hospital romance was now in full bloom. The things we did in that room with three other patients present I'll leave to your imagination.

Within a month, everyone in the hospital and rehabilitation center were aware of our budding relationship. The amazing thing was that now that I was taken every nurse wanted to flirt with me. But I wanted nothing to do with them. I was in love.

During the healing process I had a minor setback. The suture line had split apart and needed to be resewn by the surgeon.

During the procedure he asked me if I was going to be stealing Nydia from his staff. I grinned and told him that was my plan. Like I said, everyone knew.

Discharge day was the last day of winter. Nydia walked with me to the van and wrapped a scarf she had knitted around my neck. We were both misty eyed as we hugged and kissed each other goodbye. It turned out that Nydia feared that this was just a hospital romance and would most likely be the last time she'd see me again. She couldn't have been more wrong.

Chapter 18 – Bonding

The entire ride home my parents kept inquiring about my new girlfriend. They had known Nydia, the nurse, but not Nydia, the potential daughter-in-law. I couldn't get home fast enough because the parental vetting process was driving me whacky. I eventually said, "Ask her yourself. She's coming out to visit next weekend." Their jaws dropped. Finally, there was silence in the car.

Nydia lived in Queens with her seventeen year old son, Kelly. The weekend finally arrived and Nydia took the forty minute train ride to the Syosset station where my dad picked her up. During our conversations leading up to this day, I sensed Nydia was very apprehensive. My dad must have put her at ease because she was noticeably relaxed when she walked into the house. We squeezed each other firmly as if we hadn't seen each other in years and then kissed quickly. I then formally introduced her to my mom. I knew then and there that she would be easily accepted into the family.

My birthday was two weeks away and Nydia wanted to do something special to celebrate. She asked if I could meet her in Manhattan to spend the weekend together. I said of course, just tell me where and when. It just so happened my buddy Brian was dating a woman in the city so we drove in together. Every detail fell in place. Brian dropped me off at the Hilton and then left in my van. This was the first time I had been away from parents overnight since my accident. In my wildest dreams I never imagined meeting a beautiful woman like Nydia, yet alone having the chance to spend a romantic weekend together. Nydia greeted me in the lobby and after embracing we headed to our room. She was so beautiful in her dress and high heels that I trembled inside. Nydia knowing how special this evening was had made an arrangement for cheese and crackers and a bottle of champagne. For the next forty-eight hours we never left the room.

Before exiting the room I asked Nydia why me? Here is this beautiful woman who could have anyone she wanted and she chose me. She first looked puzzled. Then she said, "You make me smile, laugh and bring out feelings that have been dormant for a long time. You've touched my heart and soul like no one else ever has. When looking at you I don't see a disabled man in a wheelchair, rather a man with courage, confidence, and mental toughness with plenty to offer this world." After a few more hugs and kisses, I was back in the van with Brian. I was heading home, but grinning all the way.

Back home, my folks asked me how my weekend went and if we had taken in the sites. I replied, "Oh yeah, we saw the sites." But I'm sure we were not talking about the same thing. It was then that I announced, "I'm going to marry that woman one day." They were shocked and pleased, possibly filled with all the fears that all protective, loving parents feel, and maybe even a little doubtful. But they knew that when I set my mind on a goal, I was determined to succeed.

June was Nydia's birthday, so now it was on my shoulders to plan the celebration. I planned a three day, two night trip to Atlantic City. Since Nydia was still getting comfortable driving the van and a three hour trip would be too much for her, my mom and sister accompanied us with Susan handling the drive. This allowed Nydia to relax and enjoy her special birthday celebration. We stayed at the Resorts Casino Hotel with a stunning ocean view. The weatherman blessed us with gorgeous blue skies allowing us to stroll on the boardwalk. We popped in and out of every casino in sight and indulged in some fine restaurants. That very night I popped the question.

No, not that question silly! I asked her if she would be willing to leave NYC and move somewhere in the suburbs. To my surprise she was agreeable and loved the idea because now she could have a dog, grow a garden, and breath fresh air. I had to tell her to slow down. We first needed to find a place.

Long Island real estate was skyrocketing and the property taxes were ridiculous so living near my family and friends was off the list. My brother, Rick, lived in Connecticut and we asked him to keep an eye open for a nice condominium community. A week of viewing the real estate classified section of many newspapers elapsed without a hit. Lo and behold Rick called and said he found an ideal place. He gave me a quick summary and told us that we needed to get up there ASAP before they sold out.

That upcoming weekend, Nydia was spending the weekend with us: perfect planning. On Saturday, Nydia, my folks and I drove up to CT to check out the condo. We first stopped at Rick's for a quick pit stop and then followed him to see this community for ourselves. It was twelve miles from his house which was a comfortable distance. Close enough, yet far enough away to give each other privacy.

Driving through all the back roads, we had no clue where we were. Then Rick turned his directional lights on and we turned into the development. The name of the community was Southfield Green, in Manchester CT. Manchester is twelve miles east of Hartford, the state capital. Southfield is a private community, surrounded by a golf course and wetlands. This complex would eventually house ninety-eight units on twenty-five acres. Only sixteen units had been built at this time and the rest of the surrounding area was nothing more than a large mountain of dirt.

The ranch model we walked through was designed to perfection. It consisted of two bedrooms, two full bathrooms, a large family room, patio deck, central air-conditioning and a kitchen with cathedral ceilings. The total living space was fifteen hundred square feet. Also, the basement was as large as the main floor. It was huge. The condo deck backed up to the 6th fairway and gave us a view that was forty yards of green grass lined with a row of tall trees.

The second we walked through the condo we knew this was the home to start our new life together in. All of us discussed the pros and cons. Then Nydia and I agreed to purchase it. Turning to the real estate agent I told him we'll take it. The agent started filling out all the paper work and after signing we presented him a check for the deposit. Then we all headed home to plan the logistics for the big move. Closing and moving was set for August 20 giving us no time to waste.

Chapter 19 – Leaving NY

Packing day came twenty-four hours prior to the closing. We rented a U-Haul moving truck and my good friend Brian volunteered to help us out. Brian drove the truck into Queens and with the assistance of Nydia and Kelly loaded all their possessions. Then the three of them drove back to my folk's place. My dad and Kelly loaded my stuff and locked up the truck.

The next day, at the crack of dawn, my dad and Kelly took off with the truck. The builder was kind enough to allow us to start moving in before the afternoon closing. We slept a little later, had breakfast and got ready to leave. Before getting inside the van I took a long look around our family house. Having lived in Syosset my entire life, it was tough to say farewell. However, I knew it was time to turn the page. I was looking forward to finally living under my own roof.

Anytime we drive long distances we ask my sister, Susan, if she would do the honors. She enjoys driving and is excellent at it. My mom joined us. The drive to Manchester, CT was roughly 130 miles and would take a little over three hours. GPS systems had yet to be developed and boy we could have used one. Since we had been to our future home only once before, we got lost. We circled the area multiple times before stopping at a gas station for directions. The sad part is no one had ever heard of South Main Street. It began to feel as if we were in the twilight zone. Eventually, we spotted Rick on the side of the road flagging us down. He jumped into his car and guided us the rest of the way with Susan following close behind.

Once the van stopped, the women got out, and Rick and my dad climbed in. The entire drive to the closing, my brother, clearly annoyed and frustrated, kept asking me how we could have gotten lost. Rick was not only my brother, but my attorney representing my interests. Dad updated me on the progress of moving our belongings into the condo. He said everything was in the proper rooms and that the construction crew had pitched in. We had borrowed an old couch and folding table from Rick. Those pieces would be our kitchen and living room furniture for a few weeks.

We finally arrived at the other lawyer's office only ninety minutes late. We were directed to the conference room where everyone was pouting. Time is money to an attorney. It was a Friday afternoon and they most likely planned to be far from the office by this time. Oh well. When I saw how many documents warranted my signature my head started spinning. There were well over twenty documents. It took over an hour to sign them all. Upon completion, sore arm and all, we headed home and had our first meal on the deck: takeout pizza. Then it was bedtime under my roof. Everyone was exhausted. But I felt proud of what we had accomplished.

Chapter 20 – Settling in

The first full day in our new home, we all seemed to be in a fog. Nydia started unpacking and putting our stuff away. Kelly, Nydia's son, was busy doing the same in his room. Susan who had agreed to stay with us for a week to help get us settled, hung out with me by the pool far away from the commotion.

That night, we prioritized our shopping list so we could hit the ground running in the morning. Grocery shopping was number one on the list. The next stop was a furniture store less than a mile away. Now, I'm the first to admit that furniture shopping is not my expertise, so the women made all of the purchases. When they found something they liked I'd be called over for my advice. Having no taste in design or fashion, asking my opinion was a futile attempt to include me in the decision-making. My response was always the same, if you both like it, buy it. My expertise was haggling over the price with the sales person in an attempt to save some money. By the time we left the store we had purchased new couches, one coffee table and two end tables. Our credit card was smoking.

The following day, we purchased a dinette set with five chairs and a matching hutch. The condo was starting to resemble a home. Every day I would anxiously wait for the UPS truck to drive into our complex. It was the golden age when banks were competing against each other to gain accounts. For opening up a bank certificate of deposit, besides the eleven percent that we were receiving, three Sony color televisions, a six foot grandfather clock, a microwave oven, a boom-box and a hi-fi stereo system were included. In advance, we had carefully planned the locations for all the items. Now it was just a matter of time before our dream came true. Yet, I began to miss those good old days when life seemed simpler.

After a week, my sister had to leave us on our own and get back to her job. Now, we were down to three. Kelly was getting restless because there were no teenagers in sight. He was heading into the army that November so I suggested he apply for a job at McDonald's. It's an ideal place to meet kids his age and it would provide him with spending money. He took my advice and the suggestion came to fruition. He made friends and settled into his new home. Just as he became comfortable it was time for him to board the bus for boot camp in Oklahoma. Finally, it was just Nydia and me. For the next six months we got to play house, making adjustments to our home and familiarizing ourselves with the surrounding area. Many of my days were spent watching the construction of the other units and chatting with the new neighbors as they trickled in. Nydia spent numerous hours planting her garden.

Boredom soon set in. We now wondered what we were doing here and asking ourselves if we had made a mistake. Knowing that

I needed the advice of an expert, I gave Kelly a call. It soon became apparent that I needed to find a job.

Chapter 21 – Job hunting

One day, while listening to the radio, I heard an advertisement for Lift Inc.; yes, the same outfit that I worked for before, only the Hartford branch. Being a brazen person, I gave them a call. I assumed that since this was a different branch it must have had a different coordinator. I was wrong. Dear old Linda answered the phone. My throat tightened as I'm sure hers did too. However, she did agree to meet with me.

Seeing Linda in her office gave me the chills. The meeting lasted thirty minutes with me throwing every line of *BS* I knew in order to win her over. I thought she was leaning toward giving me a second chance but at the last moment she said no. She felt betrayed and didn't feel she could trust me again. It turns out that was the best outcome for me and one she would eventually come to regret. Rob two. Linda zero.

The next step on the job hunt was to establish a relationship with the CT vocational counselor. I gave them a call and set up an interview with a counselor named Kathy. Kathy was a tall, friendly women, who knew, most importantly, where the job openings were. During our first meeting, she immediately started looking through her rolodex until her eyes lit up. Kathy read me a job description and asked me if I would be interested. It was a programming job working on personal computers. Yes, computers were just starting to become a useful tool in the work place. The hiring company was Aetna Insurance and was located in Hartford. I jumped at this opportunity. Kathy told me she'd set up an interview and get back to me in a couple of days. I left her office feeling very comfortable that this would pan out. It did.

Kathy came through and made all the arrangements. The job was going to be on a three month trial basis with the promise of a fulltime position if I was successful. The interview was set for noon with a human resource representative, followed by a meeting with my future supervisor.

Aetna is a Fortune 500 company headquartered off the I-84 exit ramp in Hartford. The commute was easy, door-to-door, taking fifteen minutes. It is a tremendous building built in the early 1930s. The corridors were wide enough to fit two trains down the middle and still have walking room on both sides. It was an intimidating structure.

A human resource counselor met us at the security desk and signed us in. Then he escorted me into his office and asked Nydia to get comfortable on the chair outside. Since the interview went smoothly we went on to the next step: meeting with the supervisor, Mark Gelanis.

Mark Gelanis was a few years younger than I. At five foot eight, he wore wire-rimmed glasses, and was very laid back. Some people have the ability to make you feel relaxed immediately. He was one of them. After he explained what his department was working on, he said he was looking forward to me joining his team. Although most of the technical stuff went over my head and my eyes glazed over, Mark told me not to worry. That, he assured me, was part of the learning process. At that moment I knew this place was for me.

I couldn't believe my luck. Two days later I started work. My job hunting days were over for now.

Chapter 22 – Aetna (part I)

The alarm woke us up at 4:30am and our house came alive: lights on, coffee maker perking and toast popping. I was still getting the sandman out of my eyes and wondering what the hell we were doing up at this ungodly hour. Yes, it was day one of a routine we would replay every working day throughout my career. After washing, getting dressed in my shirt and tie, and being transferred into the wheelchair, we were ready to go. All I needed was my powdered sugar doughnut before out the door we went.

Mark was already at his desk when we arrived. We exchanged hellos as Nydia set up my water container and put my lunch away in the cabinet. Yes, I always brown bagged my lunch, not because I was cheap, but because it was just easier and safer than my getting sick on the cafeteria food. A quick kiss goodbye and she was gone.

It was now time for me to ascend the learning curve. My desktop sported a new IBM personal computer which was my first exposure to one. Mark dropped two manuals on my desk and told me to start reading them and to familiarize myself with the PC. He assured me that I couldn't break anything and to be adventurous.

There was a DOS manual and a Turbo Pascal programming manual. The DOS manual teaches you all the commands necessary to control the operating system on the PC. The Turbo Pascal manual teaches the syntax, functions and features of how to develop applications.

One by one, as the team members came in, Mark introduced me to them. Everyone was pleasant and they all extended offers to help answer any questions I might have. Returning to my desk I started reading the DOS manual and testing all the commands on the computer. A few hours of this and it was already lunch time. Mark and a co-worker were always kind enough to open my lunch container and set up my fork. After taking roughly ten minutes to polish off my lunch, I took a stroll around the building.

The afternoon was a carbon copy of the morning. Mark called me into his office shortly before quitting time and asked how it was going. I admitted that some aspects were understandable, while most was still over my head. He laughed and said not to worry. He continued to say he believed in me and that I would be up to speed in no time. Mark had a gift for lifting my spirits as he coached me along, a trait I'm truly thankful he possessed. When Nydia arrived she asked, as we walked down the corridor, how my first day went. I told her that my head was going to explode and we both started laughing.

By the end of my first month, I was computer literate and had started to nibble on learning Pascal. Mark assigned me my first project which entailed writing an application that could be used to calculate percentiles for compensation. After reading over the specifications I looked up to the ceiling for some divine intervention. None came. Some portions of the task I handled with no problems, the remainder my teammates helped out. Somehow the hard work paid off which impressed both Mark and me.

Around this time laptops were emerging and Mark was in charge of evaluating them for departmental utilization. Mark's desk was always swamped with laptops. He urged me to stay abreast of the leading edge technology. That philosophy carved out the path I followed throughout my career.

My last assignment during my trial period was to write an application to calculate the read/write speed of the disk drives. This was an intensive application. Completing it faster than Mark anticipated caught him by surprise. I had exceeded his expectations. This made me proud. I was finished in time for my evaluation.

Mark spent a couple of hours on my review and then called me into his office. I was looking for good news. The review covered my ability to learn new technology, work well with teammates, my attitude and attendance. When Mark was finished he said that he would bring it to his manager tomorrow with a strong recommendation to hire me. I thanked him and told Nydia the good news on the drive home.

The next morning, when Mark returned from his manager's office, he was beet-red and livid. He composed himself and sat down next to me. His manager informed him that his department had no openings and that Friday was to be my last day. He took it harder than I did. But we both agreed it sucked. He then threw something against the wall in his office and then left the office for the day. I was in shock. Explaining this to Nydia during our walk down the corridor that evening, she was understandably angry.

On my last day, the team treated Nydia and me to lunch in the executive dining room, The atmosphere felt like Good Friday and this was the Last Supper. Everyone was still distraught. After we finished our lunch, we said our sad goodbyes. Going down the corridor for the last time I turned to Nydia and said, "I'll be back here one day and when I leave it will hurt them."

Mark would later tell me he sent my resume and review to eighteen hiring supervisors, but not one offered to interview me because I was in a wheelchair. It was the first time I felt the wrath of discrimination and it made me sick.

Chapter 23 – Killing time

When the following Monday arrived, it was extremely quiet throughout the house. No alarm clock going off in the wee hours of the morning. No rush to get out of the house and into the office on time. The routine we had mastered over the prior three months was no longer needed. It felt like a weekend, but we knew better.

As easy as it would have been to sit around pouting over how I got screwed, I knew this wasn't going to help me find another job. Even though the shock hadn't worn off, I had to emphasize the positives. Knowing that I had successfully achieved all the goals, despite not being offered a fulltime job, had its silver lining. It gave my confidence a huge lift and taught me that nothing was impossible. Mark, despite that setback, had become my mentor and good friend and would continue to guide me throughout my career. Also, I now had a resume with marketable skills on it that could lead to future opportunities.

The most important commodity in life is time. We are all allocated with a certain amount on this planet. When it runs out that's it. Just because I wasn't currently employed wasn't a reason for me to stop learning. Nydia and I immediately rushed out and purchased a PC and a printer. Mark was kind enough to assist me in setting it up and loading copies of software. He continued to give me homework assignments designed to keep me sharp and busy. Good friends, like Mark, are hard to find, but worth the wait.

One afternoon, while watching TV in the living room and gazing out the window, my neighbor walked by with her puppy and yelled to Nydia to come quickly. "What is it?" Nydia asked. She rushed from the kitchen muttering a few expletives in Spanish. I assumed this was an emergency, but it was not. As soon as Nydia spotted the puppy, I knew she was instantly in love. The puppy was so cute. After the woman left, I asked Nydia if she wanted a puppy too. "Yes," she replied. I raced out the door, down the ramp and caught up with the woman. I politely asked her where she had gotten the puppy and if we could adopt one of its siblings. She answered, "You can have this one." Hmm, was this a trap all along? She explained how she had adopted it without taking into consideration the time necessary to care and train it properly. Within minutes, Cookie, our new puppy, was living in our condo: food provided and toys included. From that day on, Cookie was Nydia's first love. That left-out feeling lasted me for nine years.

Cookie was part Chihuahua and part cocker spaniel with most of his features being the latter. Most pet owners think their pet is the smartest and we were no exception. When we would leave him alone for hours he wouldn't touch his food or water knowing that making a mess was unacceptable. Just before we would leave the house, he would walk to his pillow and lay down while Nydia put his towel over him. When we arrived home, he would greet us at the door with the towel still on. At night, he slept in a television box and wouldn't make a peep until we began to stir. If we stayed up late, and he was tired, he would walk to his box and wait for Nydia to give him a boost.

Nine years later, one of the toughest nights in our lives, we had to put Cookie to sleep. It was a dreary night with light drizzle and a damp chill in the air. Our neighbor and friend, Carmine Filloramo, volunteered to drive us to the veterinary office figuring we would be too emotionally shaken. The office was empty and had an eerie feeling. Only the doctor and his assistant were there. We all went into the examining room where Cookie was placed on the metal table. The assistant inserted an IV line in his left paw where the medication would be injected. We all said our goodbyes and gave the doctor the green light. It really tugs at the heart to stare into a loved one's eyes as their life ceases to exist. We thanked the doctor and left in tears. Carmine was in worse condition than we were. *Mister Steady Driver* managed to drive over two sidewalks on the way home. . . OMG!

The house was empty and sadly quiet. The tapping sounds of Cookie's nails walking on the wood floors was replaced with those of his parents' sniffles. Everywhere we looked reminded us of our precious pooch. It took a few years before we would adopt another dog. Over our remaining years in CT we would adopt two more dogs, both beagles. Neither of them measured up to Cookie, not even close.

As the months passed more condos were occupied. In the unit three doors from ours a nice elderly couple moved in. I greeted them next to the carport and welcomed them to the neighborhood.

Their names were Dick and Ilene O'Connell and they were roughly my parents' age. We hit it off instantly. Dick and I became very good friends. Dick was the Senior Vice President of human resources for A&P. He was on long term disability due to a damaged heart and was waiting for a heart transplant. Afternoons we would have our twenty minute chat and then I'd mosey home. When things went wrong with our condo or the van he was my go to guy. Having Dick in my life was like being blessed with two fathers.

Right after the Christmas holidays, I got my big break. Every Monday, the local newspaper had an extended business section. This particular issue profiled James Lynn, Chief Executive Officer for Aetna. He was going to be the chairperson for the Hartford United Way charity drive. The article not only profiled his life story, but included his home address. Not known for being shy, I saw this as an opportunity, a direct line to the *big cheese*. Since trying to contact the Aetna CEO through the company would be an exercise in futility, this was my big chance and I grabbed it.

I turned on my PC and started typing a one page letter describing my experience at Aetna, both the positives and negatives. The overall theme explained that I wanted to come back and work for Aetna. What had happened to me in the past I stated violated the humane image that Aetna wanted to portray. With the first draft in hand, I asked my friend Dick to review it before mailing it. Dick told me that if he received this letter during his active days he would have been on the phone immediately. With that said, Nydia placed the letter in an addressed envelope and drove to the post office. There, she attached a registered/return receipt postage stamp to the envelope. Then she slid it in the outgoing mail slot addressed to James Lynn's residence.

It took nearly two weeks before the return-receipt was delivered to me, but soon afterwards the wheels were set in motion. Just as Dick predicted, Aetna's Senior VP of Human Resources called me. After cordially introducing himself, he apologized for the mishandling of my situation and promised me that I'd be back in Aetna within a week. He thanked me for my courage to speak up and fortitude for standing my ground. He ended the conversation by telling me that he was certain that I would be an asset to the company and was looking forward to meeting face to face.

Now, it was party time! Ten months of being home would soon be coming to an end. All it took was a $1.19 stamp, letter, an envelope and the proper address. By far, this was the smartest career move I have ever made in my life.

By the end of the week I received another call from human resources to come in for an interview with the VP of the Information Technologies department. The meeting was set for the following Tuesday at noon. I was more than ready.

Chapter 24 – Aetna (part II)

This department was located on the other side of I-84, directly opposite the home office. The human resource representative greeted us at the front door. He escorted us to the fourth floor, around a maze of cubicles and into the VP's office. After we went through our formal introductions, Omer, the VP, invited me into his office and closed the door. I immediately noticed that he had a Mike Eruzione original painting on his wall. Mike Eruzione was captain of the 1980 U.S. Men's Hockey team which pulled one of the biggest upsets in Olympic history by beating the Russian team and capturing the gold medal. He was elated when I commented on it and told me that he used to lock his office every night because he was concerned someone might steal it. Over time, he realized that no one would steal it since most people knew nothing about hockey. But I did. He was glad to finally have a fellow hockey enthusiast on his staff.

Omer explained what his department responsibilities were. His IT area was in charge of the installation of all the new and updated software throughout the company. His department was also responsible for evaluating all new software and hardware technologies, and demonstrating those that were approved company wide. In other words, he explained, I was going to be working on leading edge technology. My dream job had finally arrived. Omer showed me around the area and introduced me to my new boss. Then he treated Nydia and me to lunch with the promise of seeing me bright and early in the office on that following Monday. As soon as we arrived home, I gave my folks the good news. Those years of watching sports, that my mom claimed were a waste of time, had actually helped land me the job.

The first day in any new environment is always nerve racking and mine was no different. Having arrived earlier than my boss, I aimlessly strolled around my new surroundings until two people approached me asking if they could help me with something. "No," I shyly said, and then added that this was my first day on the job. To my delight, Tom and Darce, introduced themselves, welcomed me aboard and quickly made me feel at ease.

When the boss, George, a well-dressed, good looking man, finally arrived, he ushered me into his office where he reread my resume underscoring my PC skills. Since no one, he told me, on his current team had such skills, I was to be assigned all PC related initiatives. It was an ideal position and I was ready for the challenge. Afterward, he escorted me to my new cubicle where he introduced me to all my teammates. Immediately, I spotted a problem. My new workstation had some accessibility issues. My knees hit the desktop and it would need to be raised. I also informed him that my hands could not pick up a regular phone which meant that I would need a speaker phone. He said those are easy enough to fix. By the end of the day all the minor glitches were resolved.

This was the perfect place and time to be working in a research environment because it coincided with the emergence of Microsoft Windows 1.0. Aetna was on the verge of making MS Windows and MS Office the standard platform and office tools for the entire company. With this new technology there was a need to train the employees on how to develop customized applications for the Windows environment. That role fell on me and Darce. We were sent to classes to learn the C programming language and the Windows Software Developers Kit. For the first couple of months, we spent more time in class than at our desks. During this schooling, we both were reassigned to a new boss.

Our new boss, Kris, was in charge of the *consistent user interface project*. She was a little more structured than George regarding protocol and meetings. We now had to submit monthly highlights and have weekly one-on-one meetings with her. One useful bit of advice that Kris gave me was that one has to leave the company and then comeback before they are appreciated and compensated appropriately. That piece of information was filed in the back of my head and would eventually prove useful.

One day, the supervisor of the ergonomics department approached me and asked if I would demonstrate my track ball and touch pad to a group of physically and mentally challenged children. To me, that was a rhetorical question. I am always more than willing to assist others and will never turn my back on anyone seeking help. About twenty children attended and it was a blast. After my demonstration, they asked questions and tried out all the gadgets. The smiles on their faces were precious. I assured them that they could achieve anything they put their minds to. I was living proof. The following week photos of the kids and me were posted in the weekly company newspaper. On another occasion, I represented Aetna by appearing on the cover of a nationally public magazine. Oh yes, I did send a copy to Linda from Lift Inc. just to rub it in. It's in my Italian blood, I never forgive or forget.

In 1992, on Christmas Eve, alongside the tree, I proposed to Nydia. She was shocked and broke into tears as I waited anxiously for a reply. "Yes," she finally said. That Christmas day, while my brother was hosting the holiday festivities, we broke the news to the family. Everyone was delighted. I had reached yet another milestone in my life's journey. However, the celebration was short-lived. . When we returned home, I heard some wheezing in my chest. It was a bad flu season that winter and I had developed pneumonia. I spent seventeen days in Manchester Hospital where fortunately my primary care doctor was the head of the Pulmonary Department. When discharged, I joked, "If this is what happens when you get engaged, he'd better be on call when Nydia and I get married."

After five years in this department it was time to move on. I transferred to a job in the Small Business Market department located in Rocky Hill, CT. SBM provided insurance for companies with less than fifty employees. They were on the threshold of developing an automated system for their customer service representatives. Since small businesses were going in and out of business often, SBM was still paying off false claims of defunct companies. The bottom line was that they were losing millions of dollars. Our team had one mission, develop a technical solution to stop the bleeding.

I knew the technology better than any team member, but lacked the business knowledge. The development team consisted of four of us, with the leader being quite eccentric. We spent every day for six weeks in a conference room designing the system. Since I was the new member, I kept my mouth shut and my ears wide open. The longer the leader babbled on, the quicker I realized that this project was in trouble. One night, while driving home, Nydia asked how the project was coming along. She was confused when I told her I was totally lost and had no idea. It turned out, I wasn't alone. The only one who thought he knew what he was discussing was the team leader. I finally broke my silence and told the team that the proposed system couldn't be built with the software tools we were using. It was doomed for failure. I could feel the air being sucked out of the room. I was right. Two weeks later, the team leader and the second in charge were forced to leave the company.

That left me and a young Vietnamese man named Rick with the pressure solely on us to provide a solution. Pressure always energized my competitive juices and success was my only goal. In a week, we designed a new system. We became co-leaders, developed specs and hand held all the junior programmers. The two of us controlled the code library and nothing was checked in without our approval. We brought on two consultants, one to design and maintain the database, and another to help write portions of the code. The finished application would reside on customer support desks throughout the country. It was the first client-server application in Aetna and saved SBM three million in the first year. When raise time came I expected a promotion. Instead, I received a two percent salary increase. This was insulting. I discussed my displeasure with my boss, but he wouldn't budge.

During the project Rick and I became friendly with one of the consultants, Mike. A day wouldn't pass without Mike telling me how underpaid I was and that the grass was greener in the job market outside the company. Remembering what Kris once told me I decided to meet Mike's recruiter and check out my options. After meeting with the recruiter, he lined up some interviews.

While waiting to see if Mike's recruiter could deliver and still feeling unappreciated, I transferred out of the SBM department and accepted a position in Middletown. My friend, Tony, was in dire need of my skill-set and promised me my promotion. It was a good enough reason to move on.

Tony delivered on his promise regarding my promotion, but the work was boring. When Tony informed me that he was leaving the department, I knew that it was time for me to get serious about leaving also. The recruiter and I would talk every day. It was a little awkward to talk with a recruiter over a speakerphone so we had to come up with code words. If an interview went well and an offer was on the table, it was sunny out; a rejection meant rain.

Things became complicated when a mutual friend of Mark and mine, Chuck, took over Tony's position. Chuck, who was a real nice guy, told me how he was looking for my guidance on getting up to speed in this department. I cringed. I knew that my departure was imminent and wouldn't sit well with Chuck.

After interviewing with four companies I accepted a job at Shawmut Bank. I received the official offer on the Monday prior to Thanksgiving and immediately contacted Chuck. He was in total disbelief and begged me to stay. Then, before hanging up, he told me that he had to talk to his manager to discuss my departure. An hour later, Chuck called back and said he wouldn't accept my resignation over the phone. It had to be in writing and signed. Since Nydia and I always took vacation for the entire week of Thanksgiving and this year my sister was hosting the holidays, Nydia made a quick stop and delivered my notice.

Just as I predicted, my leaving Aetna would hurt them more than it hurt me. However, the saying *payback is a bitch* was double-sided because it was a friend who was feeling the pain.

Chapter 25 – Bank on it

My last day at Aetna was December 16. My Shawmut start date was scheduled for January 8. Nydia and I planned it that way so we could have three weeks off in-between jobs and enjoy the holiday season. Shawmut was located in Hartford, right off I-84. It was an easy drive and had garage parking which was a blessing in inclement weather. My boss, Peter, was a tall, thin, easy going man from England. During our three weeks off, I developed a pressure sore again and needed surgery to repair it.

Technically, I was unemployed during this period and knew my start date would have to be pushed back to the end of March. However, it wasn't the start date that kept me up that night after receiving the bad news from the doctor, but rather it was having to call Peter to explain my situation and hope the position would still be available when I returned. The one thing I feared most was to be stigmatized as not being durable and dependable. The next morning when I updated Peter, he told me not to worry and not to rush the healing process. He continued to assure me that my position would remain open as long as the recovery takes. I thanked him for understanding and told him he wouldn't regret waiting. What a great guy.

While watching the news one afternoon, in February, I heard a news flash that Fleet Bank had just taken over Shawmut. Could life get any crazier? I informed Nydia and gave Peter a call. Peter assured me not to worry since I was coming in at an officer level. The worst case scenario, he explained, was that I was guaranteed six months severance pay. Not bad, I thought, for someone who had yet to work a day there.

Healing was on schedule and my first day in the office was the last Wednesday in March. Due to the takeover, the work originally planned for me was scratched. So instead, Peter used me as his troubleshooter. If any area needed my expertise I would be loaned out. This was enjoyable and satisfying. It offered me the opportunity to learn different aspects of the business as well as meet new people.

In early August, we thought my butt was developing another pressure sore. Once again, I informed Peter that it needed five additional weeks of rest. He said no problem. Out on medical leave I went again. Fortunately, the medical crisis was averted when it was determined that I only had a rash which cleared up in five days. Where most employees would return after one week I decided to take off the entire five weeks. Peter and Shawmut were already prepared for me to be out for five so why disappoint them.

With four weeks to do whatever we wanted Nydia and I decided it would be a good time to get married. The first person I told was my good friend and next door neighbor, Carmine Filloramo. Carmine, and his charming wife Francesca, were blessed with a set of gorgeous identical twin girls. He was born and raised in Manchester and his entire family lived within a five mile radius. The Filloramo family warmly embraced us as one of them. To this day, his girls refer to us Uncle Rob and Aunt Nydia. After congratulating me he asked where we were going to hold the event. I suggested putting up a tent in the backyard. He quickly smacked me in the back of my head and asked me if I was insane. He was never one to mince words. He urged me to get in the van and ask if the country club banquet room was available. The place was ideal and a stone's throw from our home. Luckily for us it was available and we put down a deposit.

My uncle Ed, a Catholic priest based in Hong Kong, was home for a two month visit. Every three years he comes back to the US to visit his family and we were hoping he would perform the ceremony, He told us if we got permission from our local church that he would be honored. When we contacted the church and listened to the priest explain all the red tape we would need to go through before getting approval, I realized it was never going to happen. I was never a fan of all the rules the Catholic church imposes. Uncle Ed was out and my brother, a probate judge, was in.

Nydia and I came up with our list of invitees and started calling them one by one. There wasn't enough time to send out formal invitations. Whenever anyone confirmed, we would immediately take down their meal requests. We kept the reception to a manageable size with forty-six guests coming. We auditioned a recommended DJ in our backyard. He passed our test and we chose all the songs we wanted to hear. Once everything was in place, I returned back to work, the very week leading up to our wedding.

Nydia comes from a very small family and was feeling glum because her son Kelly and his family who lived in Oklahoma, didn't have the financial means to fly in to celebrate our nuptials. Secretly, Carmine and I decided to call Kelly and make all the arrangements to fly the entire family here. They flew in that Friday and Carmine was kind enough to pick them up at the airport. He hid them from Nydia and called me at work to update me when everything was ready. As soon as we hung up, I called home to tell her that there was a commotion in the backyard. She said no; it was just some little kid playing. It was then that she noticed her son Kelly. I heard her scream and the phone hitting the floor. Am I the greatest, romantic guy in the world or what?

It was Labor Day weekend and we were blessed with three gorgeous days of weather. The wedding ceremony and reception went off without a hitch. A wonderful time was had by all. Isn't it amazing how people have such a good time when there is an open bar?

Chapter 26 – Back to reality

Most of my remaining work was migrating Shawmut applications to run on the Fleet platforms. The one assigned to me was a challenge. This application was designed to provide the business support team a tool to manage Shawmut's real estate holdings. The current application included downloading data off the local database server, uploading it to the mainframe for processing, downloading the results and then finally uploading the results back to the local database. The entire process took six hours every night to complete the cycle and required a co-worker, not me, to be on call.

The next two weeks were dedicated to printing out all the source codes involved and trying to understand the logic. Once I mastered the logic, it was time to code this application. Utilizing the programming language C++ to rewrite the logic took roughly six weeks. After a few weeks of testing and debugging, it was almost ready to be transferred over to Fleet. I documented the entire process and inserted all of it into a folder. The last step was to meet with my counterpart at Fleet and walk him through the entire process. We met for two hours. Once he was comfortable with my application, he signed off and my work was finished. The developer of the old system said that it was impossible to turn his laborious six hour program into a five minute process. Confident in my application, I offered him a hundred dollars to defy my results or crash my application. He tried his best, but not a penny came out of my pocket. I had succeeded.

By the end of April, my work was done. Severance packages weren't going to be handed out until sometime in September. With nothing left for me to do, I asked my boss if I could stay home. He agreed to that as long as I was available in case of an emergency. I told him no problem. The entire spring and summer Nydia and I spent relaxing while Shawmut continued to pay my salary. Jesse James couldn't rob a bank any smoother than I had managed to.

My five month paid vacation was drawing to a close when I received a call advising of when my last day of employment was scheduled. I now had two weeks to find another job and my recruiter started lining up interviews. Within an hour he had arranged three, all on the same day.

That day of interviews started in the morning with a visit to United Technologies, a Fortune 500 company specializing in building jet engines. There were armed guards protecting drab gray buildings. There wasn't a single patch of grass in sight. If you didn't know better you would swear you were in North Korea. Ugh! I was escorted to the cafeteria and waited for the boss who turned out to be busy. In her place she sent three members of her staff. They were your typical engineering geeks in short-sleeve shirts and ties with slide rulers in their shirt pockets. Their one overriding rule was that every team member had to be on call one night a week. I told them being on call would be impossible for me. After they reiterated it was a requirement, I reached down and turned my wheelchair on and left. The job wasn't for me.

Next up, was an interview with Aetna. I arrived at Aetna in time to join my friends, Tom and Darce, for lunch in the cafeteria. Afterward, I met with the hiring supervisor to discuss the job opening. She was pregnant and her due date was close at hand. She was very interested in my credentials but wasn't going to fill the position until she returned from maternity leave. I wished her good luck and said we'll talk in a few months.

The last stop of the day was with a consulting firm, Command Systems in Farmington, CT. The first meeting was with my friend Chuck; yes, the same Chuck I had left hanging at Aetna. He was the head of human resources and held no grudges for my leaving. We talked about the working environment, compensation and then he showed me around the company. Chuck had an assignment in mind for me and asked if I would mind interviewing with the company on the floor above. The company was Kaiser Permanente, a medical insurance company. I said sure. Exhausted at this point I made sure this meeting was going to be a quick one. After greeting the four members in the room I rattled off all my skills, accomplishments, and attributes in rapid fire. Two of the members in the room I already knew me from Shawmut, but the other two were blown away. They only asked me one question. When could you start?

Since I had four more days before receiving my separation papers and severance package from Shawmut, I told them a week from today.

Chapter 27– Consulting World

I was suddenly entering the consulting business with companies now pleading for my services. Ten years ago doors were slamming in my face and now I kicked the doors down. I no longer had to settle. I had earned the right to pick and choose. My confidence level ran high, bordering on cockiness. This allowed me to negotiate my compensation in line with my equally talented associates in the field. It took a massive amount of sweat and dedication on my part by studying, networking and building a solid reputation for delivering quality results.

The assignment at Kaiser was contracted for ten months and the expiration couldn't come soon enough. The staff was friendly and treated me well. However, the work wasn't stimulating enough. During the end of this assignment, I received a call from a friend working at another consulting firm inquiring about my availability. He elaborated on the project he was working on and said they needed help. This project piqued my interest so I scheduled an interview, checked it out and accepted a job offer. Next stop CMS.

CMS was a consulting firm located in Glastonbury, CT, a ten minute scenic drive from our home. The headquarters was located in South Carolina and we were one of their subsidiaries. Headquarters had just signed a multi-million dollar contract to build an inventory tracking system for a large manufacturing company in SC. They needed as much help as possible. Overwhelmed, they borrowed five members from our team to work on the project from the Glastonbury office. They would send the specifications to our project leader and he would hand out our assignments. Every two weeks all the finished pieces would be downloaded to the main office and assembled to their place of work. We could work as many hours as we liked. Every hour after forty was overtime. I was doing sixty and my friend was pushing eighty hours. It was raining money in our office.

The money was great, but the hours were wearing down my body. The entire premise of working at a consulting firm is that they are very generous with salaries, but the other benefits are weak to non-existent. History had taught me when my body was on the verge of breaking. I knew that the place for me to be when this occurs was back at mother Aetna,. Coincidentally, one of my teammates had just come back from interviewing at Aetna and decided he wasn't interested in the position. He explained what the job entailed and was kind enough to provide me the supervisor's name and email address. Back at my desk, I quickly typed an email, attached my resume and sent it off to the Aetna supervisor. Shortly after, I got a response asking when we could meet.

Explaining to him that I used a speaker phone in the office, I asked him to call me that evening at home. On the ride home, I updated Nydia on the opportunity that my colleague dropped in my lap. She was originally taken back, but soon realized it was a smart move to make. During dinner, the phone rang and Aetna was on the line. We set up a meeting for after work the next day. The meeting with the Aetna manager, Tom, went smoothly and he wanted me on board *pronto*. When I told him that I needed to give CMS two weeks' notice, he frowned. He realized it was common courtesy and I never wanted to leave an organization on a sour note. Two weeks later I was back at Aetna. The funny thing is my desk was twenty feet from where I sat during my first stint there. I laughed thinking how far my career had traveled.

Chapter 28 – Aetna (part III)

During my first and second stint at Aetna, I was treated like a pawn. After my consulting stints, everyone treated me like a genius. As a previous manager had told me years back, you have to leave the company and then come back before you're recognized and compensated appropriately. How true that was.

Three years had passed since I last strolled down the Gothic corridor at Aetna and not a thing had changed. There were many familiar faces. It was as if time had stood still. I greeted many acquaintances on my way to the boss' office as if we had seen each just the other day. Tom, the manager, welcomed me to his staff. He then explained that his team provided technical support to the investment services portfolio managers. The portfolio managers were responsible for investing all of Aetna's monies and decisions were formulated based on the information our applications provided. There was no margin for error.

Insurance companies are restricted by law as to which financial instruments they can invest in. They must have limited risk. Aetna's holdings were in bonds, treasury notes, real estate and money markets. My first assignment was in the real estate section and it entailed developing a library type application. This would allow the file room clerks to keep track of which property analysts were checking in and checking out the folders regarding an individual property. Three months later, the program was up and running.

Aetna was beginning to phase out their real estate department which left me to spend more time in the bond investing department. It was now 1999. All work revolved around insuring that Aetna applications were compliant with Y2K. We weren't alone in this initiative; companies worldwide were also spending millions of dollars to insure their applications wouldn't crash when the clock struck midnight ringing in the twenty-first century. Data storage was extremely expensive in the early days of computing. Most dates were stored with just the last two digits of a year. The problem was applications run mathematical algorithms based on those last two digits and now there was no way to differentiate between someone born in 1900 or in 2000. Doomsayers were predicting the end of the world, but when the ball dropped in Times Square there wasn't a blip.

All my time was now dedicated to the portfolio managers working alongside my supervisor, Win. He was a technical wiz who understood the business process better than anyone else. The two of us were handpicked to work on the risk management project representing our department. At this time Aetna had no viable means to determine their investment risk leaving them vulnerable to an unexpected crisis or market crashes. This project came directly from the CEO which meant the spotlight was on us. Working closely with the portfolio managers and outside vendors,

Aetna had a system running in nine months. Win always took good care of me. At the end of the project we both received huge bonuses. When I told Nydia how much she almost drove off the road.

Not too many things rattle me, but on two different occasions an Aetna employee made idiotic comments regarding my wheelchair. The first occurred in the morning while I was strolling back from the cafeteria. A naive young woman said to me that she was exhausted and wished she had one of those, pointing to my wheelchair. Her idiotic comment left me shaking my head in disgust. Knowing a formal complaint would get her fired, I let it slide. On another occasion I was zipping through the hallway and a mature woman made a similar comment. This was alarming when you consider how many dollars Aetna spends on diversity training. I reported both incidents to human resources and explained to them that their diversity program was failing badly. She said they would look into it and thanked me for informing her of the situation.

It was October when I realized that one thing failed the Y2K test, me. My ugly nemesis, the pressure sore, reared its ugly head and literally took a bite out of my left buttock. I went to see my local physiatrist, a doctor specializing in SCI and nerve related ailments, who confirmed my greatest fear. Surgery was warranted and another three months out of commission. The doctor then asked me a question I would have never expected from someone specializing in rehabilitation medicine. Knowing me for many years and witnessing the wear and tear on my body he asked, "Why do you work?" A few seconds passed before I responded,

"Because in order for me to go out on long term disability I need a doctor to complete all the paperwork justifying it." He responded, "I have no problem with that and I will handle it." No matter how invincible or indispensable we may believe we are there will come a time in everyone's life when the body cries out no more. That time was here.

The following day I explained my situation to Win. That Friday, the team took me out for a farewell lunch. My working career was now over and. I was only forty-three.

Chapter 29 – The Lost Decade

The twenty-first century started a ten year stretch of very rough years for Nydia and me. Every time it appeared my life was starting to get on a positive roll, a medical issue would occur. This was the most mentally grueling time of my life. It tested our faith in God to the breaking point.

My medical condition was in a downward spiral and no doctor had the answer. Nearly every morning, as Nydia placed me in the wheelchair, I would begin profusely sweating. Sweating is a defense mechanism that informs spinal cord injured individuals something is hurting in a region of the body that can't be felt. It could be a frigid day or eighty degrees out. It doesn't matter. Sweat just kept pouring out. A light blue polo shirt could turn navy blue within thirty minutes. By noon, I was forced to wrap towels around my neck and wear a headband to absorb the moisture. There were only two ways for me to avoid this torture: stay in bed or tilt my wheelchair in a reclining position.

We live in the age where we expect doctors to provide a quick fix to all our medical problems. Whatever was causing my condition had the medical world perplexed and made living almost unbearable.

The first doctor we consulted was Dr. Seetharama, a physiatrist at the Hospital for Special Care in Farmington, CT. He immediately scheduled me for a complete urological work-up. Urinary tract infections are a common ailment for quadriplegics and common side-effects are sweating. The results came back negative so that was ruled out.

His next thought was that I had osteomyelitis, bone infection, in my lower spine. He contacted a neurosurgeon and arranged for me to have a bone biopsy. Not only were the results negative, but the procedure left me with a gaping wound on my back that took forever to close. Just what I needed.

The clouds over our heads were getting darker and it was time to look elsewhere. Dr. Petrillo had left Rusk Institute a few years prior and was now running his own rehabilitation center at Norwalk Hospital. Norwalk is located in southern CT, seventy-five miles from our home. I made an appointment and we crossed our fingers hoping he had the solution.

By this time, two years had passed without a resolution and despair was setting in. I updated the doctor on the past few years of hell and he cringed when I mentioned the bone biopsy. He told me no doctor should have ordered that procedure and wished I had contacted him earlier. Dr. Petrillo admitted me onto his floor. Over the next five days, he ran numerous test including a MRI and CT scan. Since my suite was huge, Dr. Petrillo allowed us to put another bed inside so Nydia could stay. It wasn't the ideal environment for Nydia, but she endured the four nights.

When the results came back negative, Dr. Petrillo decided to treat my condition with medication. He prescribed Dibenzyline three times a day. Following his advice I took the medication for a year with no results, at which time we stopped. To add to my misery, I also developed a small sore below my right hip. Dr. Petrillo decided that this wasn't caused by pressure but possibly from a bug bite. Knowing how spotless Nydia kept our home, I was skeptical of that prognosis.

As months passed the sore continued to grow larger. My doctor, Laurie Loicano, who ran the St. Francis wound clinic agreed with Dr. Petrillo's assessment. Over the next few years Dr. Laurie would become our guardian angel. Whenever we hit a rough patch, day or night, we knew we could contact her for help. She is the most caring and dedicated doctor anyone could hope for. Nydia and I were blessed she was on our team One morning the area became quite swollen and beet-red. Nydia alarmed, expressed her concern. After a call to Dr. Laurie, I was told to come in to the clinic immediately. Once she inspected the area she immediately called her partner and asked if he had time to debride the wound. She then instructed us to go straight to the hospital where an attending doctor cleaned out the infected territory. Nydia snapped a picture of the area after surgery to show me. The wound area was wide and deep enough to hide my wallet. No exaggeration! I knew this was going to need surgery to close this canyon. Ugh!

It was 2007 and I had a wound on my left buttock. My right hip was a disaster area and my Mother was gravely ill.. The only positive news was I was still alive and the sweating had decreased. Every morning and evening Nydia would change all the bandages.

A chore that took two hours out of her day. We were at our wits' end and sinking quickly into the abyss.

In early August, my sister gave us a call to inform us that Mom didn't have much time left. Susan suggested we drive down that weekend to say our goodbyes. Aware of the urgency and despite being exhausted, we drove to LI to say our farewells. I would have never forgiven myself had we not made the trip, no matter what damage it might do to my body. Our mother was dying from a long battle against lung cancer. The combination of chemo and radiation therapy had taken its toll. She was now a mere skeleton of herself. When we arrived at my sisters, Susan went to get mom dressed and the two of them met us in the living room. Due to my own medical issues, we hadn't seen Mom in a few months. I almost didn't recognized her when she was wheeled into the room. I felt as if someone had ripped my heart out. After chatting for few minutes with my family I asked if everyone could allow me some time alone with Mom. Her outer beauty was gone, but her inner strength was unscathed. I maneuvered my wheelchair carefully alongside her and placed my hand on top of hers. Looking into her eyes I noticed a tear running down the side of her face. Extending my arm as far as I could reach, I was somehow able to wipe that tear onto my sleeve. Mom then mumbled a couple of things to me. Though unable to understand the words, her message came across loud and clear. Mom was saying her final goodbye. I understood how proud of me she was for never quitting, happy that I had found and married such a lovely woman who she knew would love and take care of her son forever, and elated that I had grown to be a productive member of society. During the three hour ride home there was very little conversation between Nydia and me.

Losing a parent is difficult enough, and every day is precious. As painful as it is to say, Mom was ready for a better place. Three days later the cell phone rang. It was Susan again. No words were necessary. The greatest mother in the world was now pain free and in God's hands.

It was now the holiday season and the medical system was grinding to a halt. Dr. Petrillo and I finalized our strategy for repairing my wounds. I was scheduled to be admitted on the first of March to his rehab floor. The following day my hip wound would be surgically closed. After recuperating from that, my butt would be operated on next. Three months later, God willing, I'd be back home and wound free.

That was the plan. *What really happened was a fiasco.*

Chapter 30 – The Main Event

Muhammad Ali named his heavyweight fights the *Thriller in Manilla* and *Rumble in the Jungle*. Mine was called the *Nightmare in Norwalk*.

The weeks leading up to our trip down to Norwalk exhausted me. Within an hour of sitting up I would fall asleep, something I had never done before. My speech sounded slurred even though Nydia and Carmine assured me that it wasn't. My ankles and abdomen were swollen. Something serious was brewing. March 1 couldn't come fast enough.

It was a typical cold and dreary morning in CT when we embarked on our ninety minute drive to Norwalk. Within fifteen minutes, I was sound asleep and had to be woken by Nydia when we arrived. That would be the last thing I remembered over the course of the next seventeen days, not because I was unconscious, but rather I have erased those days from my memory.

Based on Nydia's recollection this is what transpired. The staff, whom we both knew from previous admissions, greeted us and a nurse's aide escorted us to the suite. Nydia quickly started organizing the room, unpacking our bags, and cleaning any dirt in sight. Then a couple of aides lifted me onto the bed and undressed me. The nurse followed and took vital signs and asked questions regarding my medications and medical history. When she finished, I got comfortable and Nydia headed down to grab a bite in the cafeteria.

As Nydia was walking down the hallway, she spotted Dr. Petrillo and Dr. Silverman, my plastic surgeon. As she got closer she heard the doctors discussing my next day's surgery. After saying hello, she reminded them that I had been taking an aspirin a day for the past year. An aspirin regiment causes the blood to thin, making bleeding more difficult to stop. The doctors looked shocked, even though the aspirin was listed in the forms we had provided. Hearing this news, Dr. Silverman postponed the surgery for a week.

Nydia, hungry and exhausted, still had the foresight to remind the doctors about something so elementary that they should have known, but she assumed they didn't. She is always thinking of everything the doctors should be aware of in order to protect my well-being. If the surgery had taken place as originally scheduled, I would have never made it off the operating room table. Was this divine intervention or Nydia's thoroughness? I believe it was both; and this saved my life.

Our four week stay now turned into five. Dr. Petrillo used those days to determine what was causing the swelling. Sadly, the answer came the hard way when I went into full blown respiratory and congestive heart failure. In a twelve hour span I went from a hundred and sixty pounds to two hundred. A fluid buildup. I was rushed off to ICU.

The medical terminology for my condition was hyponatremia. The patient's sodium level drops below a certain range and the fluids in their body starts to drown them internally. Sixty percent of the human body consists of water and all of mine was collecting internally. The process of raising your sodium to a normal range is a slow process. The staff couldn't simply push an IV of sodium based fluids into my system to solve the problem.

Since I was now unconscious and laboring to breath, I was intubated. My condition was listed as critical. Once again, God had placed me at the crossroads between life and death. Nydia was by my side almost twenty-four hours a day, questioning every medication, procedure or anything else, no matter how minor, that happened in my room. Her devotion to my well-being was overwhelming. Love knows no bounds.

My sodium numbers started to improve and the medical team decided to remove the tube. Immediately, my numbers started dropping again. A decision was made to re-insert the tube but now that I was conscious, I refused. Each time a patient is intubated makes it more difficult to remove them from the ventilator. Given everything Nydia and I had been through in our lifetime, being dependent on a breathing machine for the rest of my life wasn't going to happen. I was still the master of my fate no matter what the hospital staff recommended.

This refusal put the staff in panic mode. Dr. Petrillo repeatedly tried to convince me that this was in my best interest, but again I said no. He then turned to Nydia and tried to persuade her on my behalf. Knowing my wishes, she stood her ground and told them no. Her courage to resist such pressure was remarkable even if it meant losing me.

Failing to convince us to change our decision, Dr. Petrillo left the room in tears. The team's next option was to have a psychiatrist interview me to determine if I was mentally competent. The psychiatrist began questioning me as the staff anxiously watched through the glass window. After I lucidly answered all of the questions to her satisfaction, she informed the staff that they needed to find another solution. To this day, I can't recall any of the questions or my answers.

In frustration, the pulmonary department recommended placing a CPAP mask over my face and forcing oxygen into my lungs. CPAP, or continuous positive airway pressure, is a treatment that uses mild air-pressure to keep the airways open. It typically is used by people who have breathing problems, such as sleep apnea. Sticking your head out of a fast moving car is the exact sensation you get from CPAP. Somehow, against the best medical advice, this worked, finally putting the discussion of intubation to rest. Yes, it was a risky gamble, but one that God allowed me to win.

Could this nightmare get any stranger? It sure could. As my sodium level was slowly improving, my mind went wacky. All the doses of various medications they gave me turned my mind into a state of psychotic paranoia and me into a mean-spirited bastard. My mouth was running nonstop and anyone who came into my room would be subjected to being verbally lambasted, including Nydia and my family. This was the exact opposite of my usual demeanor. The drugs were stronger than my will. Added to this irrational behavior was the psychotic effects the drugs had on me. They catapulted me into a hallucinatory state where everything going on in that hospital seemed to be an actual episode out of *Mission Impossible* and the staff were mere actors. I was lost in the abyss.

After fourteen days in the ICU, the decision was made that it was time to return me to the rehab floor. This was the wrong decision. I lasted only three hours in my room. No sooner had Nydia gone to the cafeteria to eat a quiet dinner, than my room was swamped with nurses and other specialists. My aide, who had brought my dinner tray, discovered that I was unresponsive and unable to speak. I blankly stared at the ceiling, my mind in a catatonic state. The team assumed that I had suffered a stroke and called for an immediate brain scan. When the results came back negative, I was taken straight back to ICU.

I suffered from a condition called Sundown Syndrome. It occurs in the late afternoon or early evening. The condition can include increased confusion, disorientation, agitation, depression, paranoia and rapid mood changes. This necessitated yet another week in ICU until the effects of the drugs wore off. Dr. Petrillo came to visit me on a Sunday morning and asked me what I wanted to do next. I replied it would be nice to return to his floor for a few days and then go home. That afternoon I was back on the rehab floor.

That first night, I had trouble sleeping. I was afraid that the catatonic beast would attack again. When sunrise came I thanked God. The beast was gone for good. The plan was to leave in two days, barring any setbacks. But would this nightmare finally end? No. The morning prior to leaving, the nurse came in to take my vitals. My pulse was running high so she decided to take an EKG. After she read the results I knew, from the frown on her face, that something was wrong. She walked out of the room and then reemerged with others following right behind. I muttered now what? The answer came quickly, my heart was in atrial fibrillation. Atrial fibrillation, also called AFib, is an irregular heartbeat, or arrhythmia, that can lead to blood clots, stroke, heart failure and other heart-related complications.

Needless to say, I was now placed in the cardiac unit. The cardiologist spent two days testing different medications trying to convert my heart to a normal sinus rhythm. After all the medications failed, they went to their last option, the paddles. In my room came the crash cart, a couple of cardiologists and a nurse. They first administered some Propofol to put me in a light sleep, then placed the paddles on my chest and zapped me. No effect. The shock level was raised and I was zapped away. Again, no effect. Cranking the level even higher, they zapped one last time. Still no effect. I awoke to learn that this cardioversion procedure had failed. Everyone left the room with their heads bowed. I was brought back to rehab floor for three more days before I was permitted to leave for good. Thirty days into this nightmarish experience and I was heading home in worse condition than when I had entered.

Departing day was a picturesque early spring afternoon with bright sunshine, blue skies, and not a cloud in sight. Once I had passed through the sliding doors, the sun radiated off my face and my lungs filled with fresh air. Feeling alive and free, my emotions got the better of me. I broke down in tears with a combination of emotions: thankfulness that God and Nydia had saved my life and allowed me to see another day; joy that I survived this whole ordeal; bitterness, because the medical staff had failed to detect these ailments before they became out of control; shame for being such a monster and treating everyone like shit; and last, guilt that I had put the woman I love through so much mental and emotional anguish. Nydia had endured more than any person should in a lifetime. Yes, my mental state of mind played a major role but somehow I should have had the strength to overcome that.

At this moment, Nydia told me, *suck it up and let's get the hell out of here*!

Chapter 31 – Heal Thy Wounds

We had a restful weekend, in our own bed, before starting down the road to good health again. Monday afternoon, I met with my local cardiologist, Dr. Korkmaz. He reviewed all the paperwork Norwalk Hospital had faxed over and listened to my tales from the crypt. He then had his nurse join us in the examination room to assist in taking another EKG. He summarized his findings. The AFib was still present and he wanted me to see a specialist, Dr. Tolat at St. Francis Hospital. Prior to leaving the office the secretary had already arranged my appointment to see Dr. Tolat that Wednesday at noon.

Dr. Tolat was a specialist in cardiac electrophysiology. He studies the electrical activity of your heart to find where an arrhythmia, the abnormal heartbeat, is coming from. These results can then help him decide whether you need medicine, a pacemaker, an implantable cardioverter defibrillator (ICD), cardiac ablation or surgery to correct the problem.

We arrived promptly and were directed to an examination room. The nurse followed us and started jotting down my medical history. She left for a split second and returned with the EKG machine. She then hooked it all up, and ran a quick test, but still there was no change. Before she could finish her next sentence Dr. Tolat walked in to review my EKG. He explained that the reason for my constant fatigue was because my heart was beating three times faster than normal. He compared it to running a marathon every day, day in and day out. Then he explained the procedure he wanted to perform to correct my irregular heartbeat.

It is called a catheter ablation. It is the least invasive option. The doctor puts a thin, flexible tube into a blood vessel in your leg or neck which is then guided to your heart. The doctor then uses heat, cold, or radio energy to scar some tissue inside your heart, where the irregular beats are triggered. The treated tissue helps get your heartbeat back into rhythm.

Fear set in and I nearly passed out. Dumbfounded that this was happening to me, I asked him who else has had this procedure done. He told me Senator Bill Bradley and Prime Minister Tony Blair to name a few. That was good enough for me. He asked his nurse to find the first opening on his schedule. She came back and said Friday at 2pm. Stupidly, I told the doctor that I couldn't make it that day because I had tickets to *The Phantom of the Opera* on Saturday. He chuckled on the way out and said, "I'll see you Friday."

That Friday I was prepped and ready for the procedure. A scope was placed down my mouth to check for any blood clots. After I was cleared, the procedure was scheduled to begin. However, there was one more hurdle. I refused general anesthesia. I wanted to be awake for this procedure. I was still the master of my fate. The procedure went smoothly and was successful. To test the results, the doctors tried to shock me back into AFib. When he couldn't, we knew I was on the road to recovery. Instantly, I was feeling ten years younger.

This procedure doesn't work on everyone. God's shining light was getting brighter and the gloomy clouds over my head were finally clearing. With a healthy heart, we could now move on to address the wound on my hip and my buttock.

Chapter 32 – Momentum

The success of the ablation was a huge boost to the household morale. We were now seeing the light at the end of the tunnel. Yet, Nydia and I were not sure if we could have handled another setback. The hip was next.

It was now July 2009 when I returned to St. Francis Hospital to have the hip wound surgically closed. Dr. Brown, an older gentleman, was the plastic surgeon. The operation went as smooth as butter. I spent five days in the hospital and another three weeks in bed before I was back up and on the go. The area was finally closed for good. The world was looking brighter each day. Two down, one to go!

Even though my hip surgery was successful I wasn't very comfortable with Dr. Brown. It was his age that concerned me the most. Yes, older doctors usually have more experience but they also have shakier hands. Unfortunately, I didn't follow my instincts and allowed him to surgically close the wound on my left buttock. My poor decision would come back to bite me in the ass.

Three months had passed since my hip surgery and I was

about to enter the operating room again. The surgery went as planned. Four hours later I was resting in my hospital room. The following day, when the nurse was examining the surgical site, she noticed a small opening. She inserted a Q-tip in the opening and realized that it was more than superficial. It had depth. I would spend two months in bed hoping that it would fill in. It never happened. The surgery was botched. When we attempted to contact Dr. Brown, or arrange an appointment he was nowhere to be found. I believe it was the last time he operated out of St. Francis.

It would be another year until I would attempt the surgery again.

Chapter 33 – Getaway

After everything we had been through over the last decade, it was time for a long vacation. Winter was approaching. It was the ideal time to head south. We rented a condominium on the ocean in Singer Island, Florida for the months of February and March. Two months of glorious sun and fun sure can rejuvenate one's spirits. On a rare occasion, a light sweater was enough. Otherwise, it was always short sleeve weather. It was paradise!

My sister, the best sister in the world, was kind enough to take some vacation time and drive us down. When we arrived two days later, we were anxious to see our rental unit. It was on the twenty-third floor with a stunning east view of the ocean. We enjoyed ourselves so much, we bought a unit on the eighth floor and closed four days prior to leaving.

Over the years, while vacationing in Florida, Nydia and I have done our share of house and condominium shopping within a ten mile radius of West Palm Beach. We viewed numerous luxurious properties before settling on our condo. Our decision was based on two factors. It was on the ocean and my dad lived in the adjoining building since 1999. Since my dad was aging, we wanted to spend quality time with him and provide as much support as possible.

My dad, now on the verge of turning ninety-two, was once the rock of Gibraltar. He was a soldier during the invasion of Iwo Jima in World War II, the father of three children all of whom graduated college and went on to successful careers, the union president at Sperry looking after his co-workers, and the man who guided me through a tragic situation

This was our time and opportunity to pay him back for everything he had done for us. The first couple of years in Florida were easy since my dad still had plenty of pep in his step. This past year has been more difficult: physically and mentally for my dad, and emotionally for us. His body is failing, his footsteps reduced to a virtual crawl, and his mind slowly drifting away. As age continues to take its toll, he can rest assured we will be there for him.

In the four days we had remaining, we cleaned out all the antiquated junk, bought new bedding and installed two flat panel televisions in our new condo. We then handed the keys to our real estate agent asking her to list it as a rental until we returned the following January. She got lucky and found us a tenant for ten weeks. The rent covered the expenses while we were gone. Every penny counts.

The drive home was the last time we would make the twelve hundred mile trek on I-95 by car. I told Nydia from now on the only way we are traveling to and from Florida was by air. Susan, Nydia and I started our journey home early in the morning and it was already eighty degrees. When we stopped in Delaware the second night it was thirty. Ugh. Back home it would be another ten weeks before we would see eighty on the thermometer.

I was certain that we should be living year round in the Sunshine State. Nydia was not yet convinced.

Chapter 34 – Leo

Back home it was now time to try again to close the remaining wound on my left buttock. Working closely with the Dr Laurie, she recommended a top notch plastic surgeon to repair the area, Dr. Leo Otake. He had recently left his practice at Yale to work at St. Frances. Listening to Dr. Laurie's advice, we chose Dr. Otake to repair the mess his predecessor had created.

Surgery was set for early December. This would provide us with enough time to recuperate and still allow us to get down to enjoy our new winter home. It was late October when the northeast got hit with an unusually early severe ice storm, downing power lines and causing havoc for days. Luckily, my sister had power and backup generators so we packed up and headed to LI. This storm convinced Nydia it was time to leave CT.

Dr. Otake did a marvelous job and the wound was finally sealed. Doctors rarely throw their colleagues under the bus, but I had to know if it was my fault that the wound never healed or Dr. Brown's. When I asked Dr. Otake his facial expression answered my question. I would spend two months healing at the Hospital for Special Care and it snowed nearly every other day. Roofs in the area were buckling under by the weight of the snow. When I was transported home, I noticed our roof had at least three feet of white powder resting on top. I promptly told Nydia, "Run and get out of the house if you hear a loud crack." I was serious. There was no sense of both of us being trapped.

Chapter 35 – The snow birds

Nydia was skeptical of us flying down to Florida. She was afraid that my wheelchair would get damaged in the cargo compartment. I designed the ultimate plan and convinced Nydia to give it a try. If all the items on my agenda worked as planned this would go like clockwork. There was no room for failure or I would never hear the end of it.

First, we hired a friend of Carmine's, John Ryan, to drive our van. We loaded it with my everyday wheelchair, clothes and medical supplies that we would need for four months. When he arrived in FL on the second day, his job was to unload everything into our unit and enjoy the night. The following morning, we rented a van and used a manual foldable wheelchair to get to the airport. With the assistance of a few bulky JetBlue employees, I boarded our flight and was securely transferred into the front-row aisle seat. The remaining passengers then boarded. When we approached the runway and the pilot went full throttle, I was like a kid in the candy shop. It was awesome.

There is nothing sweeter than going from snowed in Manchester to sunny West Palm in less than three hours. The crew transferred me back into the wheelchair and John was waiting at the departure exit. He handed us the keys and we handed him his plane ticket home along with a check for his services. This process would be repeated two more times, all flawlessly.

We now had four months to organize our home. Every single item from the previous owner was either thrown into the garbage or donated to charity. The appliances were the first to go, replaced with stainless steel. Then we bought a new dining room table and chairs. Next came a new bedroom set and mattress. Mercifully, we stopped there and focused on picking out the tile and grout for the entire condominium.

Heading into our last week of vacation, Nydia didn't want to leave. Every day she quietly pouted, but knew we had to go back north to sell our Manchester home. Besides, the tile was going to be laid that following Monday, leaving us no choice.

Back on the big bird, we were heading home with a busy agenda: pack our belongings and sell our condominium.

Chapter 36 – Moving time

We had spent thirty years in Manchester with no regrets. Many good times and friends were made over that three decade span. We were finally in good health and no longer wanted to tolerate the five months of gloomy winter weather. The thought of operating two homes was too difficult and expensive. Florida was the easy winner when comparing the cost of living, weather impact, no state income tax and an extremely generous reduction in property taxes for individuals in my condition. The only thing we would miss were our friends, Carmine and family (who did eventually move to Florida the following year), Ken and Nancy Laro, and the close proximity to my sister.

When you live in one location for three decades it is amazing how much you accumulate. Nydia was in charge of the packing and I handled the selling portion. The game plan was simple. If it didn't fit in a box that could be shipped via UPS, or fit in our van, it wasn't coming with us. The number one mistake northerners make when moving south is hiring a moving company to ship their furniture. Storage facilities are full of furniture that owners have brought with them, just to fade away. It is cheaper to buy all new furniture that fits your present decor.

Nydia started by packing her crystal dolphin collection. Then she sorted the clothes with those that were going and those to be donated. Every time we had three boxes packed, it was UPS time. Our kind neighbor in Florida would slide them into our unit. The furniture was sold on consignment or through Craig's List. Ken received our broken grandfather clock, which he fixed. It now resides in his dining room. The remainder of my baseball cards and memorabilia I gave to two young boys, Yankee fans, who resided across the street. They were giddy and very politely thanked me. Before we knew it, we had reduced our furnishings to two beds, two televisions and a kitchen table.

I was in charge of advertising and selling our home. Most find the easy way of selling their home is to hire a real estate agent and let them do all the work. Not me! There was no chance a realtor was going to gobble six percent of the proceeds while I'm alive. That's a chunk of change that was better off in our pockets than some realtor's. Our home was immaculate and had the prime location in the association. We knew it would sell quickly.

We started by creating fliers and handing them out to all the residences in our community. The association board, who frowned on my breaking the *no solicitation* rule, slapped me with a warning. Promising not to do it again was enough to placate them. The fliers brought in four prospective buyers. It was easy to pick out those that were serious from those who were just being nosy. These four fell in the latter category.

Needing to reach a larger audience, I placed a three day ad in the Hartford Courant that ran over the weekend. When the newspaper arrived, our phone started ringing off the hook with potentials buyers. By the end of the weekend, we had one couple on the hook. I just needed to slowly reel them in. They attempted to haggle the price down but we wouldn't budge. The good news is they bought our home and wanted to take possession as soon as possible.

Nydia and I were planning on an early October exodus; they wanted it in early September. We compromised. The closing was in the middle of September.

Manchester, thanks for the memories.

Chapter 37 – The Sunshine State

Florida welcomed us with open arms. We knew this is where we belonged. In our few years down here, not one moment has passed that we regretted our decision. Everything moves at a more relaxed pace and the people seem friendlier than up north. Since this is going to be our last move, we took our time unpacking. My motto became, born on an island and will eventually die on one too.

After the initial tile was placed throughout the unit, we remodeled the kitchen, replaced all electrical outlets, switched all doors to six panel with new hardware and had the walls painted. The following year we remodeled the bathrooms. We are proud to call this home.

The gated community we reside in has twin buildings containing eighty-eight units in each and is twenty-four stories high. We're on the eighth floor with a western exposure. Our view features the boats on the Intracoastal, stunning sunsets, and the city skyline of West Palm Beach. There are four units on each floor and we share a washer and dryer. Most of our time is spent outside sitting around the pool, the club house or on the private beach. All are within a three hundred foot radius. The island is five miles long and a less than a mile wide. The ocean side of the island is lined with high rise condominiums and the Intracoastal side with individual homes. The entire island is a hidden gem in southeast Florida. Nydia and I have a saying, if someone has to live in paradise it might as well as be us.

Even though I stopped working in 2000, living in Florida is the first time it has felt like retirement. With our health issues behind us, we now have the time and energy to enjoy the finer features that life has to offer. Besides the occasional medical appointment our calendar is blank. We come and go as we please and answer to no one. Dining out is more the norm than the exception. Outdoor concerts, movies, theatrical plays and gambling excursions fill our time. We can watch the world go by.

One piece of advice, when you are lucky enough to retire have some hobbies to keep you physically and mentally fit. This allows partners to spend time apart which is extremely healthy. Two hobbies that keep my mind competitive and my juices flowing are managing our portfolio and playing poker at the casino.

Managing our financial portfolio is a hard gut-wrenching job. Most would allow a money manager to handle this task, but I enjoy the hands-on challenge. Our household mornings begin to stir around seven. Within seconds, CNBC is on the television and I'm glued to it for the next two hours. I'm checking what happened in overnight markets and listening to so-called experts give their stock predictions. Once up in the wheelchair, the laptop goes on and the work begins. Most days no action is taken, other days I'll buy and sell the same stock in the same day. This is known as *flipping*. The remainder of the portfolio is diversified and rarely touched.

My other adrenalin boost comes from playing *No Limit Texas Hold'em* poker. Playing online can teach you the fundamentals, but nothing prepares you for playing it live. The first time I sat across from eight others caused me to have heart palpitations. That pounding in my chest has worn off, but the excitement hasn't. Everyone at the table has one objective, to take as much money from each other as possible. Overall, I hold my own, but I still have much to learn. One thing is for sure, you won't see me on television competing in the World Series of Poker anytime soon.

Despite one major mistake, our first three years in our new locale have been marvelous. This setback occurred on the Saturday after Thanksgiving when Nydia and I spent the evening out listening to a local reggae band. The band was lousy and dusk was setting in so we decided to leave. The wind had picked up as it does on Singer Island. The flag was flapping viciously and we were moving at a rapid pace to escape a cold front. When we got to the wheelchair cut-out ramp to cross the street, I was distracted for a split-second. Before I knew it, my wheelchair was rolling off the sidewalk. I tipped forward and hit the pavement with a thud, my legs now wedged under the wheelchair. The combined force and weight of the chair broke both my legs. Thank God, Nydia's quick reflexes prevented me from smashing my face onto the hard pavement. Since I have no sensation in my legs, I didn't realize the severity of my injuries. Two gentleman helped untangle my legs and get me settled in the wheelchair so we could continue home. It was only when I noticed that my heart was racing and sweat was pouring out, typical symptoms that quadriplegics feel, that I knew that something was terribly wrong. Autonomic Dysreflexia had set in causing my blood pressure to sky rocket and the danger of fatal stroke to be imminent.

It was only after Nydia transferred me into bed and took my pants off that she understood the magnitude of what had happened and called 911. Soon after an ambulance arrived and transported me to the area hospital where the emergency room x-rays confirmed Nydia's diagnosis. My left femur, the thigh bone, and the right tibia, the lower leg, were broken. It was determined that surgery was required for the femur while the tibia would heal naturally. Five screws and a metal rod had to be implanted in the femur. This kept me in bed for five weeks.

Forty-three years confined in a wheelchair and this was my first spill. Hopefully, it will be my last. No one said life would be easy, but it sure is worth fighting for.

Chapter 38 – The Platform

When Nydia and I first moved to our paradise island home there was one change to the association property that warranted modifications. The access to the beach was restricted by a narrow ten foot Trex pathway that ended abruptly in the sand. Tropical plants and shrubs lined both sides of the path making it impossible for anyone in a wheelchair to get a clear view of the ocean. This obstacle curtailed my ability to feel like a member of the community. At our first association meeting I presented my dilemma to the condo board members. A few narrow-minded owners fought to prevent my access, but to no avail. The board approved my request unanimously and a few months later the addition was complete. The association extended the walkway another thirty feet, with a 10' x 10' platform and benches. Now, everyone, even those that argued against it, enjoys it.

On those rare occasions when I am seated in my wheelchair before dawn I'll race down to the platform with coffee mug in hand to await the sun rise. In that glorious moment, as the first few glimmers of brightness appear, goose bumps appear on my arms. Then everything goes quiet. The sun, now scarlet and blazing, rears its fierce breathtaking orb above the horizon where it meets the ocean as if the two were one and indivisible. Then, as the sun breaks free and is totally visible, it looks down on itself now reflected perfectly in that vast mirror of ocean. I shout Hallelujah, knowing that its brilliance is also reflected in my eyes. Sometimes, if I'm lucky enough to experience this with a loved one or a good friend, we break into a collective smile. Sharing this moment is priceless.

During the off-season, this is where I go to relax and contemplate. My view of the beach and ocean is as far as the eye can see. Looking to the north and to the south I can watch everyone sitting in their cabanas or frolicking in the water. On occasion, I might spot a dolphin leaping or the tail of a shark in the warm tropical ocean. Staring east I can see the point where the ocean meets the horizon. Container and cruise ships slowly pass by. When the feeling overtakes me, I recline in my wheelchair to gaze upward at the big blue sky, to reminisce of times past, to reflect on the present and to plot the course for the future.

Prime time, January through March, is when the platform takes on a new dimension. Around 2pm, my three snow bird friends hold court with me and we implement our daily briefings. Our foursome consists of Bob, the coach; Carlo, the pizza man; Steve, the professor; of course, me, the mayor. Shortly after I arrive, Bob comes lumbering down with coffee mug in hand. He has just risen from his sacred afternoon nap and is ready to start the second part of the day. Carlo is next, just getting home after his morning round of golf and an afternoon bite to eat. By this time Steve has seen us gather, he rises from his cozy cabana and begins his slow walk to join us.

With all of us situated, it is time for the brain trust to solve the world problems. All subjects are open for discussion. A fun time is had by all. Meetings last from sixty to ninety minutes, weather permitting. Since we are constantly being interrupted by those coming or leaving the beach, we have implemented the three minute rule. The rule states, any one person not interesting to the group should be encouraged to move on within the allotted time. On rare occasion when we meet an intriguing person, he or she is designated with honorary guest status for the day. Once the shade engulfs the entire platform the meeting is adjourned and we all return to our spouses, all of whom ask the same question: What did you guys talk about? We all give the same answer: *nothing*. *Seinfeld* was onto something. May our show run longer than his sitcom.

Chapter 39 – Sunset

As my arms begin to fatigue from typing this book, one keystroke at a time, I catch myself gazing out the window to watch the sun set in the west. The colors sparkling in the sky are breathtaking. Describing these colors would do no justice to one of God's greatest creations. This pause allows me to give thanks to the Almighty Lord for allowing me to enjoy another day.

It would have been fantastic to end the book on a high note by explaining how stem cell research found a miracle cure to repair damaged spinal cords. Unfortunately the shackles have not come off and a cure has remained a mystery. One reason it is taking so long is that administrations under Ronald Reagan, George H. Bush, and George W. Bush put a moratorium on stem cell research. That was a loss of twenty years of research. Who knows what could have been discovered with two additional decades of research. A cure for Alzheimer's, dementia, and spinal cord injuries? Maybe even cancer? We'll never know. If you have a loved one suffering from a one of these life altering afflictions maybe you'll keep this is mind the next time an election comes around.

My heart believes there will be a cure someday, but not in my lifetime. But that's okay. I pray for it every night, not for my sake, but so that those affected with spinal cord injuries don't have to ride such a bumpy road through life.

Chapter 40 – Why

Whenever I meet new people, young and old, they always ask me what happened. After listening to the *Readers Digest* version of my trials and tribulations, friends and strangers alike are in awe of my story and suggest my putting this down in words. This past summer turned out to be the ideal time to do just that. My objective was to type one page a day and see where it takes me. Writing this brought back many fond memories and some horrific events. Every day since the accident, I have been consumed with making it through the day, one day at a time. Now, the written word has provided me with an opportunity to take a step back and reflect on the past and look forward to the future.

Did I do everything perfectly? Absolutely not. There were no self-help books on managing life after becoming paralyzed, especially at sixteen, when a young person's body is already going through enough changes. We all live and learn. If I listed all the things that I should have done differently, it would be endless. However, I did do it my way. As hard as it might be to believe, life worked out just fine for me. Everything I planned on accomplishing in my lifetime has already been checked off my bucket list. I graduated high school and college, married my devoted wife, lived under my own roof, had a very successful working career, and now reside in a gorgeous retirement community. The one glaring exception is that I never became a father. This wasn't in God's plans.

Now I can add to the list that I have written a book, a book meant to inspire others and to show gratitude to all who helped me. Inspiration, I know is a vastly over used word. However, if I can inspire you, whoever you are, if I can awaken, challenge, and motivate you to persevere through life's struggles, then I have accomplished everything and more. I can testify that life can be a bitch, but, as they say, it sure beats the alternative. Everyone is unique. We are all born with something unique to offer. God grants us the strength to conquer obstacles that we may think are impossible. Whoever you are, don't quit. Ask for help. Don't go it alone. Others were here for me. Close friends and complete strangers will help you if you are open to it.

I'm happy that I've had this chance to offer my gratitude to those mentioned throughout this book. Life is like building a house. Before construction begins, an architect draws the blueprints that guide the developers. I was blessed with great parents. They were my architects. They taught me right from wrong, the do's and don'ts, and how life works. Nydia is the foundation. She has always been by my side. She is the rock that made all my accomplishments possible. A strong foundation never cracks and neither has our love for one another. The cornerstones are my sister. Susan, Joseph Maneri, Carmine Filloramo and Brian Landau. All four have always been there for me through the good and rough times at different stages of my life. The other individuals mentioned throughout have all played major roles in my life. I thank God every night for blessing me with such an ensemble of fantastic people. Without them, life would have been unbearable. Throughout my adventurous life, my belief in God has never waned. Who am I to challenge the path He chose for me to travel on?

One day, the good Lord will deliver the final knockout blow. I will be ready, but by no means am I rushing toward it. When that day comes, no tears please. Just say a prayer, point to the sky, and ask Him to take care of your friend.

Until that day arrives, every morning I say to myself, *Life is good!!.*

Gallery

(First row, second from left. Sitting to my left is Carole.)

(1973 Syosset H.S. Basketball....shooting.)

441-51 South Main Street
Manchester, Connecticut 06040
September 15, 1987

Aetna Life & Casualty Company
151 Farmington Avenue
Hartford, Connecticut 06115

Attn: James T. Lynn, Chairman and Chief Executive

Dear Mr. Lynn,

    After reading the article about you in the Business Weekly section of the Hartford Courant I received the impression you are an intelligent, warm and caring man. For these reasons I feel you are the one that should hear my story if you could spare me a few minutes of your precious time.

    My name is Robert Guliani and I was employed at Aetna from 12/29/86 to 3/24/87. Due to a swimming accident when I was sixteen I'm confined to a wheelchair. Being a new employee in training I was assigned to the FMD systems micro-support unit to demonstrate my ability to potentially fulfill a permanent position with Aetna.

    As my trial period was winding down I was evaluated by my manager (Mr. Mark Gelinas, Administrator, FMD Systems, PFSD, AA40) from whom I received high reviews and a strong recommendation, for the company to hire me as a permanent employee. After hearing this I was on cloud nine until, several days later when Mr. Gelinas informed me he did not have a position available and neither did all of Aetna. Mr. Gelinas then circulated a memo to all the other managers in the FMD area hoping one of them would have an opening. I have attached a copy of this memo. However, he did not receive one single response. For the first time in the past 14 years I felt like people may have been judging my wheelchair rather than my abilities to perform the job. Personally it made me sick!!! I do not believe this is the image both you and Aetna would want portrayed in the community.

    With my successfull performance record at Metropolitan Life and Aetna I find it very hard to accept that a major company the size of Aetna does not have a position for a person with my skills. I'm enclosing to you an updated resume. I pray to God that you can light a fire under those that are responsible so that I may one day return to Aetna to continue my career where I thoroughly enjoyed my brief period of employment.

    I thank you from the deepest part of my heart for your time and effort. Thank you and God Bless.

                    Sincerely,

                    Robert J. Guliani

ENCLOSURES: Memo
             Resume

(The letter that launched my career.)

(Demonstrating adaptive technology to a group of physical and mentally challenged kid's. The most gratifying day in my working career.)

(Hanging out with Jimmy Buffet at Jones Beach in 2012.)

(The greatest day of my life!!)